# THE
# *Conscious*
# STYLE
# GUIDE

# THE
## Conscious
# STYLE
# GUIDE

## A FLEXIBLE APPROACH TO LANGUAGE THAT INCLUDES, RESPECTS, AND EMPOWERS

## KAREN YIN

Little, Brown Spark
New York Boston London

Little, Brown Spark
Hachette Book Group
1290 Avenue of the Americas, New York, NY 10104
littlebrownspark.com

First Edition: May 2024

Little, Brown Spark is an imprint of Little, Brown and Company, a division of Hachette Book Group, Inc. The Little, Brown Spark name and logo are trademarks of Hachette Book Group, Inc.

The publisher is not responsible for websites (or their content) that are not owned by the publisher.

The Hachette Speakers Bureau provides a wide range of authors for speaking events. To find out more, go to hachettespeakersbureau.com or email HachetteSpeakers@hbgusa.com.

Little, Brown and Company books may be purchased in bulk for business, educational, or promotional use. For information, please contact your local bookseller or the Hachette Book Group Special Markets Department at special.markets@hbgusa.com.

ISBN 9780316478540
LCCN 2023949232

Printing 2, 2024

LSC-C

Printed in the United States of America

*For my friend and accomplice Henry Fuhrmann,*
*a.k.a. Hyphen Killer*

# CONTENTS

# Contents

Contents

# AUTHOR'S NOTE

This book contains sensitive language for the purpose of study and clarity, including slurs, stereotypes, and references to death, abuse, suicide, and sexual assault.

# INTRODUCTION

Many of us want to "do our part" in the fight against social injustices. Using inclusive terminology—or comprehending it—has become a necessity in many arenas of life. But the world of inclusive terminology can be more maze than amazing. How do we know when a word needs replacing? Who has the final say when people disagree? And why is it so hard to let go of certain words?

Though many friends and colleagues have asked me to write a book, I struggled with the idea. I knew that a reference that was essentially a menu of words would be outdated before it hit the presses. After all, language evolves. But during the process of studying language, conversing about language, and editing language, I had an epiphany. What people need more is a system— their own style—for thinking about these constantly changing issues.

Style is simply expression. Like the "fashion" meaning of style, language style is flexible and adapts to the occasion. And like fashion, your style and approach should fit you. Without a clear way of thinking, there can be no clear way of doing. So I decided to write a reference book that helped people nurture their own conscious philosophy.

I love reference books. In my youth, I read dictionaries and encyclopedias. As a writer, I pored over thesauruses and visual dictionaries. As an editor, I sought refuge in grammar books and style guides. I blogged about Associated Press style and Chicago style on APvsChicago.com for anyone "who gives a dollar sign, ampersand, exclamation point, and pound sign about style." For three years, I wrote the style column for the beloved but now-defunct *Copyediting** newsletter. Meanwhile, to perform my editorial duties, I scoured the internet, searching for online resources. Journalism affinity groups, like the National Association of Black Journalists and the Asian American Journalists Association, had published community-centered style guides to counter the recycling of stereotypes and non-conscious narratives in the media. GLAAD, the National Center on Disability and Journalism, and other organizations that support specific subcultures offered their own media guides. Despite the proliferation of resources out there, I knew from conversations with my fellow editors and writers that awareness of them was almost nonexistent. In 2015, after more than two decades of editing professionally, I launched Conscious Style Guide at ConsciousStyleGuide.com.

ConsciousStyleGuide.com was the first website dedicated to conscious language. My mission was to help writers and editors become more aware—of words, yes, but also portrayals, framing, and representation. I also launched a monthly news roundup, later named *The Conscious Language Newsletter*. What differentiated ConsciousStyleGuide.com from mainstream guides at the

*Copyediting* was founded in 1990 by Mary Beth Protomastro under the name *Copy Editor*.

time was its ability to quickly evolve. If a piece of writing had an illuminating perspective, I added it. If a resource became outdated, I replaced it. To publish a newsletter every month, I reviewed hundreds of articles to find news, opinions, and observations related to conscious language that would help my subscribers — and myself — make informed decisions.

To many, conscious language consists of kind, inclusive, and bias-free words. To me, the one who coined the term, this is an oversimplification, like reducing rainbows to seven colors. Conscious language is a philosophy and a practice that goes beyond terminology. I chose the word *conscious* because it means "aware, mindful, and intentional." So, to use conscious language is to be more aware, mindful, and intentional about how we treat ourselves and others through language. While the use of contextual and impact-conscious language is not new, capturing its many forms in a single term is. Now many industry leaders have adopted my term to describe their own inclusive language practices.

Conscious language liberates instead of limits. It emphasizes the importance of context and critical thinking, and it flexes and grows alongside society. In this book, I share my insights for building a personal practice. My favorite definition of *practice* is "translating an idea into action" (Vocabulary.com). To help you translate conscious ideas into consistent action, the chapters — Prepare, Plan, Practice, Pause, and Persuade — mimic the journey someone new to conscious language undertakes.

In chapter one, Prepare, I explain my philosophy of conscious language, who uses it, and when. After introducing the five core components of conscious language, I distinguish it from language that is nice, overinclusive, or politically correct. Then I give an overview of known limitations.

In chapter two, Plan, I discuss implicit bias, the signs of bias activation, and how we can shift our perspectives. I include a series of tips designed to reveal possible motivations, interests, and boundaries for your practice. After explaining how thinking like an editor can shape your approach, I demonstrate the importance of deferring to credible sources when questioning language.

In chapter three, Practice, I present best practices for when you are in doubt. These overarching guidelines can help you identify and remedy bias at four levels of content — word, sentence, story, and series (meaning any number of related pieces). I round out this chapter with a section devoted to conscious design and images as well as tips for respectful interpersonal communication.

In chapter four, Pause, we take a detour. Here, I address common doubts. To encourage compassion for one another, I talk about the many ways that words and beliefs may be misaligned and how to work across differences. Because working with language and dealing with people can be stressful, I provide step-by-step instructions for one of the most effective techniques that you may not know about for alleviating stress. Then I cheer you on with words of inspiration from people I admire.

In chapter five, Persuade, I outline ways to spread conscious language, including building your own stack of reference works and creating a style sheet.

How you flesh out your theoretical framework is up to you.

*Introduction*

This book exists to affirm that conscious language is a choice and that your unique voice belongs in this movement. I hope my guidance helps boost your confidence in discerning song from noise. Please marinate in the ideas set forth in this book and allow the most resonant conscious language principles and practices to illuminate your path. Ideally, you will explore approaches that are doable and reasonable and, above all, make sense to you.

In truth, this book is as much about you as it is about conscious language. Being clear about your beliefs and boundaries will help you recognize when someone else's concerns may have supplanted your own. The best person to make sense of where your intentions and goals intersect is you. Your passion for conscious language may falter if you need to pretend to be someone you are not. Our choices must be grounded, down to the bedrock, in something we believe in. If we build a practice around fear — of criticism, of exclusion — then we tend to do the least to get by. Fear may also produce piecemeal style decisions severed from throughline and thought. Curiosity, not compliance, is the way forward.

As you can imagine, it is tricky to write a guide to conscious language. No doubt, by writing a book that describes and prescribes conscious language, I am invoking Muphry's Law. As hinted by the cheeky spelling, Muphry's Law states that any criticism of a writing or editing error will contain such an error. In the process of exhorting a language of compassion and context, I am bound to make missteps and be unskillful in my choice of words and incomplete in my efforts to include. I hope that you can be charitable in your reading despite these flaws.

Also, some of you may wish that I took the guidance further, prescribed more, laid down the law. But I am consciously outlining a philosophy that can spread. For it to spread, it must be flexible. Though I present considerations for best practices, my brushstrokes are necessarily broad. Content and context work together, so rather than one-word-fits-all solutions, I encourage you to observe and explore different approaches to equity-based language so you can come to your own conclusions about what is more effective for you and your audience. My main intents are to help you close the gap between spectatorship and ownership and to provide tools for processing the shifts in equity-oriented language.

Again, this book is an invitation to think and question, not to perform. If you seek straightforward guides to terminology, I invite you to treat ConsciousStyleGuide.com as a companion to this book.

If you work with conscious or inclusive language in a specialized field — journalism, publishing, counseling, higher ed, medicine, science, the nonprofit sector, to name a few — this book can help you solidify your style, embrace flexibility, and use the power of context to effect change.

Finally, if you are looking for a history lesson on sexism, racism, and other types of bias, please visit your local or online bookstore. I touch upon identity, culture, and privilege because power dynamics are inseparable from language, but these complex concepts are beyond the scope of this book. Nor do I debate, for example, which identities are "real," whether a group exists, or why oppressed groups deserve compassion. I encourage you to read widely, especially points of view you disagree with. After all, a willingness and openness to learn (and unlearn) is essential to the idea of thinking critically about language.

When I proposed this book title, *The Conscious Style Guide: A Flexible Approach to Language That Includes, Respects, and Empowers*, my editor, Tracy Behar, thought it was imprecise. Did I mean that the approach includes, respects, and empowers, or that the language does?

I said both.

Thank you for letting me be your guide into the rewarding, joyful, and powerful world of conscious language. Please take from this book what you need.

# BEFORE YOU BEGIN

In the words of Thich Nhat Hanh, "Sometimes even the most skillful words can cause pain. That is okay."[1]

As you grow more confident in using language as a tool for equity, it is important to be realistic. Conscious language does not magically prevent us from inflicting harm. There are no guarantees that conscious words, stories, and presentations will have the intended interpersonal, social, or legal impacts. Falling short is not a reflection of your beliefs or commitment but a sign that you are finding your way around.

When our efforts feel inadequate, it is an opportunity to inquire, reassess, pivot, or reaffirm our choices. The best we can do is guide our language in the direction of social good and repair. The least we can do is forgive ourselves when we fail. Expecting perfection of yourself and others, or believing that perfection exists, is unrealistic and unsustainable.

The reality is, even those of us who have embraced conscious language will disagree vehemently on what is appropriate. We will have our own ideas about who and what matters. We will encounter people who think our most conscious language, our best versions of ourselves, is the most objectionable. And that's OK. Pushback is feedback. We can't learn if we cease to try.

Make no mistake: None of this is easy. We all have

attachments to language that may diminish our openness to change. Rather than dismissing the intimate ways our lives, identities, and understanding of the world are bound up with words, let us identify these blocks to change so that we can work with them, work around them, or accept them.

By presenting conscious language as flexible, sustainable, and creative, I hope to counter the perception that using language with care means adhering to a set of rules. Experimenting with language and different approaches encourages us to cultivate thoughtfulness and sensitivity while strengthening our self-expression and social connections. Larry Yang, a core teacher at the East Bay Meditation Center, wrote a prayer of aspiration that beautifully conveys the wisdom of continually reaching. In offering it below, I would like to invoke its self-compassion, bring Thich Nhat Hanh's words of forgiveness full circle, and send you on a conscious language journey of your own making.

May I be as loving in this moment as possible.
If I cannot be loving in this moment,
    may I be kind;
If I cannot be kind,
    may I be nonjudgmental;
If I cannot be nonjudgmental,
    may I not cause harm;
And if I cannot not cause harm,
    may I cause the least amount of harm possible
              —Larry Yang, *Awakening Together:*
        *The Spiritual Practice of Inclusivity and Community*

# THE
## *Conscious*
# STYLE
# GUIDE

## CHAPTER ONE

# PREPARE

Automatic language is the bane of conscious language. When we communicate without thinking, such as offering unwanted health advice, telling someone they are weird, or mistaking a long-haired boy for a girl—all of which I have done—we are probably not grounded in intention. Disrupting automatic language takes practice, so my goal in chapter one is to help you prepare a foundation for conscious language.

It is a lot like preparing a bed for a garden. When we clear the rocks and weeds and enrich the soil, our seeds have a greater chance of taking root and flourishing. The more flexible we are with circumstances beyond our control, the larger our capacity to withstand bad weather and other antagonistic forces. As worn as a garden analogy may be, it's a simple reminder that taking greater care at an early stage can save time spent shoring up gaps later on.

## What Is Conscious Language?

Conscious language is language that promotes equity.

The words *conscious* and *equity* are doing a lot of work.

*Conscious* means "aware, mindful, and intentional." *Equity*, at its essence, means "fairness." So conscious language connects awareness to fairness, philosophy to practice. Ultimately, it is about freedom. When words, phrases, and stories fail to affirm our humanity and individuality, we are not free. To harness the power of words for equity, we need to activate our curiosity and considerateness. Conscious language, therefore, is rooted in critical thinking and compassion, used skillfully in a specific context.

For me, using language consciously means stretching the commas in my thought process into em dashes to gather clarity and purpose. In a world that rewards binary judgments, hot takes, and knee-jerk reactions with hearts and likes, pausing to reflect can be a restorative act. Through words and narratives that include, respect, and empower, we can make room for more of us to thrive.

The truism "Words have power" may strike you as lackluster if you've heard it before, but the phrase itself is powerful. It reminds us that we, the users of words, have power. You may not think you have a say in the shape and direction of language, but every time you use a word, you vote to keep it alive, and every time you don't, you vote to let it die. Those with bigger stages and sway have bigger responsibilities to use language consciously, but we all have a say. Few acts are as rewarding as choosing language for inclusion and justice.

Conscious language has five core components: content, context, consequence, complexity, and compassion. Together, they differentiate conscious language from other styles of thoughtful language.*

## Content

What do you wish to communicate? Whatever your intention or desired impact, your message requires content. As a society, we lean on content to convey meaning, because it is the most concrete and discrete part of communication. Content is what remains, while the rest of the context forever evolves.

So, what is content? Picture a blank page. Anything you add to it, apart from the coffee ring and donut crumbs, is content. Words and images count as content. On a web page, audio and video do too. *Content*, really, is anything contained, as in the contents of a cup, a bag, a list, your mind. But that's too broad for our purposes. Here, I will focus on spoken and written words, from formal to informal, used in interpersonal communications and mass media, in a US English context. While this is still broad, I invite you to extrapolate and adapt the guidance in this book so it suits your needs.

So, content can be a single word, like *stop* on a road sign; or it can fill a book series, like Terry Pratchett's forty-some-book Discworld. When I explain my zoom-level methodology for analyzing bias in chapter three, thinking in units from word to series will be useful.

---

*Other styles that may overlap with but are not the same as conscious language include inclusive language, mindful communication, Nonviolent Communication, wise speech (also known as *right speech*), and civil discourse.

Many factors go into creating content. When skillfully done, it is more than stringing words and punctuation together. Words can effect positive or negative changes within ourselves and others. We can use language to reach into minds and shift perceptions.

In a word's lifetime, it can pick up meanings and associations that depart from its original intention. It would be fair to say that one of the primary qualities universal to language is that it is intensely personal. The words *I love you* map across our hearts with varying intensities. In each of us, this sense of *love* can broaden or constrict depending on what occurred last night, who we are meeting later, how the sun is shining, what we ate that day.

This is expected, that rills and rivulets of nuance feed the ocean of language. Consciously and unconsciously, we imbue it with shades from our interactions, triumphs, and traumas. However, as individuals, we can control the direction of language as much as we can control the tides. Which is to say, we will have a smoother time if we learn to swim.

Ideally, we create content with specific goals in mind. For example, when I wrote ad copy, adhering to the creative brief was imperative. A brief spells out the objective (the problem you are solving), target demographic (the population you are marketing to), medium (the platform used for distribution), brand narrative (the tone or persona), and challenges (potential pain points).

Knowing our audience can help us tailor our content and anticipate the success or failure of jargon and jokes. When we communicate in person and in small groups, we have the precious advantage of being able to continually modulate our words, intonation, pitch, volume, facial expressions, and body language in a harmony-seeking micro dance. And when the audience is unknown or too large—an issue I am grappling with as I write this book—the difficulty of creating effective content rises exponentially because the possible intersections of identity, society, and culture have no limit.*

Content is the sum of all its facets, which can become tools in themselves. Many experienced writers manipulate facets of content subconsciously, like a chef who forgoes measuring but continually tastes as they cook. Facets include the following (some will be further addressed in chapter three, Practice):

- **Goal:** to inform, to persuade, to educate, to inspire, to entertain, etc.
- **Level of formality (or linguistic registers):** highly formal (restricted, as with ceremonies), formal (restrained, as with strangers), moderately informal (polite, as with acquaintances), informal (casual, as with friends), highly informal (intimate, as with family)
- **Persona (or voice):** individualized style or expression
- **Tone (or attitude):** happy, harsh, jocular, timid, determined, etc.
- **Power dynamics:** honorifics, etiquette, adult to child or child to adult, boss to employee or employee to boss, etc.
- **Linguistic markers:** accents, dialects, colloquialisms, vernacular, register-switching, code-switching, multilingualism, etc.

---

*My solution is to write with a specific audience in mind while adjusting the terminology for a broader audience.

- **Social markers (cues that convey identity, culture, and subculture):** age, gender/sex, sexual orientation, race/ethnicity, socioeconomic status, etc.
- **Audience:** niche, pain points, barriers (accessibility), target demographics

Using conscious content means using words that skillfully include and exclude, with more of the necessary specificities and fewer of the unnecessary ones. Knowing your audience can help you target the ideal niche. Being inclusive means understanding the true denominator connecting your potential customers within the niche. For a luxury car, for example, the primary market consists of consumers at a certain intersection of age, interest, income level, and geographic location. But if you target only a specific gender or race, you may inadvertently drive prospective buyers toward a competitor who does not.

In everyday communication, we rarely get this fancy. We just talk or write. That is usually enough. But when the occasion calls for us to slow down and communicate with greater care, we can pull these content tools into service. Understanding our desired impact can help us choose a style that sends the intended message.

## Context

A word is never just a word. It is everything around it and then some. Being mindful of context can help us understand and influence how language is received.

Every perception of an object is influenced by the object's

surroundings. A red rose at midnight appears black. Plain water after a dill pickle tastes sweet. A piano key sounds dissonant when played with its neighbor. Likewise, a word's meaning can be changed by the words, society, and history that surround it.

Without context—a point of reference—words are no more than a jumble of marks or utterances. The word *is*, when surrounded by a *k* and an *s*, becomes *kiss*. The word *kiss* in the United States means "pee" in Sweden. *Kissing up* in an office is different from *kissing up* someone's neck in the bedroom. Context is the connective tissue that imbues content with meaning. As linguist John Rupert Firth noted, "You shall know a word by the company it keeps."[1]

That's why I believe that context is everything, and everything is context. When we take words at face value without considering the influences of people, past, and present, we are missing part of the story. If context is whatever surrounds the word, then context includes the other words, the topic and the presentation, the communicator and the receiver, history and circumstance. By consulting and adjusting context, we can sharpen our attunement to patterns and more efficiently align impact with intention. Content and context work together, so a change in context can change the meaning of the content and, therefore, the way it is received. For example, contronyms such as *gnarly* have contradictory senses—*gnarly* meaning "cool" or *gnarly* meaning "bad"?—that are made less gnarly (we hope) through context. We can also change the content to change the context. I like to reply to requests written in corp-speak with casual language to cue that it's OK to be less formal with me. However, when corresponding with a new client or colleague, I usually wait for them to signal a context change, often by way of emoji.

In lieu of a frame of reference, we supply our own. The word *tuck* by itself can trigger associations with bedtime, swimming, plastic surgery, or drag queens. Just as with optical illusions, our brains rush to fill the contextual gaps. But as with optical illusions, we can easily imagine something that is not there. So, although words may appear identical, we need to look beyond them to grasp the impact and intent.

Although we may discuss language in terms of its potential to promote harm, no word is inherently harmful or healing. Insults, like *ho* and *bitch*, can double as endearments. Endearments, like *honey* and *bestie*, can double as insults. Context can turn *slut* into an empowering identity, *girl* into infantilization of older women, and *lady* into a slur to shame men. It may be empowering to practice discerning benign words said in a pejorative tone from words widely believed to be harmful.

A word or narrative that is prima facie offensive can be softened, explained, or otherwise justified by putting the context to work. After all, context is the main difference between a photo of a nude and a dick pic. Without enough context, we scrape meaning from our history with that word. The reverse is also true: A benign word can be made uncomfortable by context, like describing stage lighting as "squint-inducing" in a review of a K-pop show on Broadway, which recalls anti-Asian caricatures, or using the word *niggling*, which approaches the *N*-word, in an article about Black people.

Our entwinement with language is precisely why good intentions alone are not enough to prevent our words from inadvertently provoking unwanted reactions. Receiving a declaration of love may be thrilling for you but threatening to another. Language is embedded with our selves, and the same word, story, or conversation can leave two people with reactions as opposite as north and south. Perhaps you have reread a beloved book, only to be horrified by the stereotypes that had somehow escaped your notice earlier. But the book did not change. We, the context, did. And though we may not have been alert to certain misrepresentations, those affected by them surely noticed. Different audience, different impact.

It is important to note that some content may be unsalvageable despite skillful development of context. The infinite, invisible, constantly interacting layers of context surrounding every piece of content make it challenging, but not hopeless, to communicate with one another. Context, then, is the constellation of factors that influence the interpretation of any word, including the following, which I simplify as "people, past, present."

### *People:*

- **Source (also communicator or storyteller):** Are you an appropriate messenger for this content? How will who or what you are affect the reception?
- **Receiver (also audience):** Who is included or excluded from the intended audience? Who is your unintended audience? Are the language and subject appropriate for this group?

*Past:*

- **History:** Are you relying on stereotypes, clichés, stock characters, or tired narratives? Do you describe only people, appearances, behaviors, foods, etc., that you perceive as not "normal"?
- **Patterns:** Which type of person tends to be the hero, the victim, or the villain? Are certain words reserved for members of certain social groups?

*Present (a.k.a. circumstances):*

- **Delivery method:** Is the message more effective in person, by phone, by email, or by text? Will the story be received better as a book or podcast? Which social media platforms will help the idea spread?
- **Length:** Have sensitive words or ideas been given adequate space to arc, transform, or resolve? Is the message better suited to a bumper sticker or a lengthy missive?
- **Timing:** Does your content ignore a recent traumatic event? Is this an ideal time to deliver the message?
- **Point of view:** Through whose lens or POV is this being shown? What perspectives are underrepresented?
- **Surrounding words:** Do the words as a whole create unintended imagery? Do the surrounding words change a word's impact? Does the context justify or support sensitive words or topics?

The biggest variable is the audience. Each reader, each listener, each audience member arrives with a rich inner world that bends their lens. We meet each word with varying degrees of charity and malevolence. In short, communication is a crapshoot. But conscious communication can help us establish trust as we make bids for connection.

In our daily lives, many of us leverage the power of context with great care. Inserting *Sent from my iPhone* in an email that was actually sent from a laptop can help excuse bluntness. Establishing a friendship with a new acquaintance before disclosing private information about yourself may demonstrate awareness of timing. Giving and getting sexual consent can make an otherwise illegal encounter legal. Sometimes no amount of context is enough to neutralize the most volatile topics and terms. But by honing our contextual awareness, we can make choices that promote inclusivity, respect, and empowerment.

## Consequence

Words have the ability to shift perceptions and impose conclusions. Synonyms, like *child, juvenile*, and *youngster*, press different buttons in us and evoke subtly different reactions. So imagine the incredible power of words when wielded with the intention to insult or invalidate. But also imagine how easily words can unintentionally place limitations on people's potential and their freedom.

Unintentional discrimination is discrimination. While intentions are important, impacts may override good intentions. For some of us, prioritizing impact may feel upside down. After all, we didn't mean that—they took it the wrong way! But selecting words for impact is exactly what poets, playwrights, novelists, copywriters, copyeditors, and other wordsmiths do. Writers have forever employed the *oo* and the *aah* of vowels, the clack and mush and hiss of consonants, the rhythm and syncopation of syllables, and the very feel of the alphabet in our mouths to fill stories with mood, imagery, symbolism, and foreshadowing—on top of the words' contextual meanings. So imagine the impact, often subliminal or subconscious, of repeatedly associating neutral words with a certain group, like the commonplace practice of reserving *spunky, nurturing, hysterical,* and *emotional* for women and *decisive, dashing, rational,* and *cocky* for men. (For implicit biases and bias activation, see chapter two's "Disrupting Implicit Biases" on page 41.)

The same writing techniques can be used to minimize harm and promote healing. Through words, we can shape thoughts, introduce concepts, and change minds. We can install barriers, encourage harmony, or seed hostility. Language that emphasizes individuality and humanity can help us avoid derogatory narratives. Thinking consciously and critically is key to anticipating consequences.

### The Power of Words to Limit

Casual exclusionary language and behaviors, commonly known as *microaggressions,*\* are often born from good intentions. Asking a person of color *What are you?* is often a genuine expression of

---

\**Microaggressions* was coined by Harvard University professor Chester M. Pierce in the 1970s.

curiosity about their roots, but the consequence may be to un-intentionally other them. Telling someone that they are attractive *for their age* is often an attempt to curry favor or reassure, but the consequence may be to unintentionally suggest they are not attractive otherwise. Joking to someone in a wheelchair that they are *sitting down on the job* or *going to get a speeding ticket* is often an attempt to connect, but the consequence may be to unintentionally reduce them to one detail.

Some critics of inclusive or sensitive terminology may scoff at testimonies to suffering, such as the idea that microaggressions can contribute to poor mental and physical health. But blaming marginalized people for "allowing" others to make them "feel bad" is inconsistent with the core values of our society. Emotions play a crucial role in our lives. Our legal system, the stodgiest of environments, has long been receptive to the idea of emotional harms. Intentional infliction of emotional distress (IIED) is a tort law that allows victims to receive compensation for emotional injury. Victim impact statements allow victims to describe the emotional, physical, and financial impact of the crime for the purpose of assisting the judge in sentencing. The inseparability of emotions and our health is not in debate.

Emotions show up in our nation's history in other life-and-death ways. Fear, anger, and disgust are the bonemeal-rich soil in which sexism, racism, disablism,* and other inequities flourish. Do people with the most power and privilege hold themselves

---

*A. J. Withers's article "Disablism or Ableism?" (https://stillmyrevolution.org/2013/01/01/disablism-or-ableism/) persuaded me to use *disablism* instead of *ableism* to emphasize prejudice and discrimination based on disability, not ability.

accountable for having these negative emotions? It seems to me that when emotions are mocked, it isn't that emotions are unimportant but that the people they belong to have been deemed unimportant by the larger society.

That said, language that exhibits prejudice may result in more than negative emotions. Casual speech that invalidates has cumulative effects that can result in myriad negative health consequences, including depression, low self-esteem, and heart disease. Not only do stereotypes affect access to housing, healthcare, education, and employment, but they can hinder self-actualization and steer people away from roles, jobs, and partners that would affirm their sense of self. Limited identity categories in the US Census have produced flawed demographics that policymakers then use for decisions and the allocation of federal funds. History books that present slanted perspectives can plant misbeliefs that go unchallenged for generations. Narrow definitions in law, such as defining rape as a crime committed only by male perpetrators against female victims, make it difficult for others to seek justice. Race- and class-neutral language can disguise the intent to incarcerate Black and brown people by criminalizing the activities associated with them.

The power of words to harm does not stop there. Dehumanizing language is a known precursor to genocide and has been used throughout history to fuel "us versus them" mindsets and justify human rights violations. Nazis called Jews "rats," "bloodsuckers," "parasites," and *Untermenschen* (subhuman). Turks called Armenians "dangerous microbes." Hutus called Tutsis "cockroaches." Colonizers of North America called Indigenous peoples "savages." In the United States, enslavers called enslaved Africans "property"; the Roosevelt administration disseminated propaganda that described people of Japanese descent as disgusting, inscrutable, and fearsome. Referring to people as animals, property, or diseases casts them as nonhuman, subhuman, or quasihuman—in essence, not people.

Ideologies of hate continue to spread today. Former president Donald Trump described certain undocumented immigrants as "animals" who "pour into and infest" the US.[2] Former presidential hopeful Mike Huckabee compared Syrian refugees to an *E. coli* outbreak.[3] US representative Steve King called immigrants "dirt."[4] Singer Morrissey called Chinese people a "subspecies."[5] Filmmaker Joel Coen grouped Black people and Chinese people together with Martians.[6] These attitudes proliferate among law enforcement officers meant to protect and serve, with immediate, often deadly, consequences: Border patrol agent Matthew Bowen called migrants "disgusting subhuman shit" and "mindless murdering savages" and later pleaded guilty to intentionally hitting Antolin Lopez Aguilar, a migrant, with a truck.[7]

And plenty of regular folks get in on the act. Some of us don't blink when unhoused people are stereotyped as *junkies* and *degenerates*. Journalists warn us to *brace* ourselves for the *flood, surge,* or *tsunami* of *illegal aliens*. Our criminal justice system labels people with the crimes they were convicted of, preventing them from integrating into society long after they have served their sentences.[8] The examples are endless.

Right about now, you may be thinking this does not apply to you—you don't use dehumanizing language. But any language that denigrates a group or individual as other than fully human has the potential to dehumanize. I've done it myself, and I have not always recognized when it was done to me, because everyday exclusionary language normalizes social inequality. Calling an Asian American worker a *machine*, telling vegetarians they are *lower on the food chain*, gloating over *getting some pussy*—these portrayals are part of a process of slow dehumanization that starts by drawing lines with words.

## *The Power of Words to Liberate*

The good news is that we have the power to shift entrenched attitudes, especially our own. We can show respect by using people's names, personal pronouns, and self-labels. We can choose terminology that includes, spotlights, or centers historically excluded groups. We can give credit to creators whose contributions have been erased. We can contextualize current affairs by connecting them to historical events. We can balance the voices and representation in our course syllabi, conference panels, and journal articles. We can reframe educational issues, like saying *opportunity gap* instead of *achievement gap* to shine a light on the need for support and resources at the institutional level. And we can explore empowering language for ourselves—conceptualizing *mental health* as *brain health* to destigmatize mental illness[9] or *losing weight* as *releasing weight* to lighten the energy.[10] Or we can identify as an *athlete* instead of an *exerciser* to push ourselves.[11] There are many respectful, creative, joyful ways to replace everyday exclusionary language with everyday inclusionary language.

By using conscious language, we can reframe the discourse and change the way people view one another and the world.

Conscious language is no panacea for societal ills, but it is a key part of creating a more harmonious future. Letting go of outdated language today can help us avoid reenergizing dangerous beliefs tomorrow.

## Complexity

Exclusionary language. Stereotypes. Slurs. What if I told you that these can be tools for equity?

The name Karen has become "a symbol of racism and white privilege," as *The New York Times* puts it.[12] A person of any non-Black race (but usually White) or gender (but usually a woman) can be a Karen—that is, a hate-spewing, space-intruding, police-reporting bigot. As someone named Karen, I fully support the use of the Karen archetype to highlight discriminatory actions against Black and brown people for engaging in common activities. Is it a slur? Absolutely. So why do I support it? Because right now, it does more good than harm.

People, situations, and relationships are inherently complex, so complexity is part and parcel of language. *Defund the police* was a powerful rallying cry for overdue racial justice. But in certain contexts, it was unclear. Does *defund* mean disbanding the police altogether or reducing and reallocating the funds for more effective measures? The slogan *Believe women* bolstered a public reckoning to take women's allegations seriously, but for many, including women, its broad sweep lacked logic and nuance.

But the snappiness of both messages was hashtag-friendly and brought a different social niche into the fold, helping to raise public consciousness about chronic societal issues. Are these slogans conscious? Maybe. The answer is not binary.

When I first began to give conscious language my full attention, I did not have an efficient repository or method of critique for the ever-changing terminology. Unless the proposed or prescribed language resonated in a personal way or was logical from my editor's perspective, most everything went into one of two buckets: do or don't. In the beginning, this system worked fine. The do/don't system is no-nonsense and easy to follow, and who among us does not want ease? Critical thinking takes work and can slow us down. So I hesitate to discourage beginners from the do/don't system, because it is an effective gateway to deeper involvement and a more textured understanding.

But, as I soon found out, the exceptions were endless, the do/don't method unsustainable. Do use person-first language to place the person first. But many disabled people champion identity-first language. Do use *survivor* instead of *victim* to acknowledge empowerment. But some victims abhor the *survivor* label, and not all victims survive. Don't use *guys* for women, because that makes men the norm. But some women, myself included, accept *guy* and *guys* as gender-free in many contexts.

Clearly, the do/don't system is not rooted in reality, because no group has one single take. To engage thoughtfully with "people words," we must reject the rigidity of contextless dos and don'ts. Rules devoid of nuance are a hallmark of zero-tolerance policies. If liberation is the goal, then nuanced practices—such as the defusing of slurs through reclamation, the welcoming of diversity in self-labels, and the exclusion of many to highlight a few—are critical. Failure to appreciate the gray areas (tip: they are all gray) can diminish our capacity to hold as valid more than one scenario. To respect our individuality and diversity of thought, emotions, and behavior, it is time to consciously make space for more complexity.

Recognizing complexity is crucial to healing the rifts in our society. It destroys the myth that a group of people has a single story, or that all activists toe the same line and all critics share one agenda. It teaches patience for language that deviates from the current ideal, as well as a healthy suspicion of politically correct language that may do harm in the long run. It reminds us to keep our minds open, hear people out, see other points of view. Most important, the multilayered impacts need time to unfurl; they cannot be manipulated like an on-off switch.

Complexity nourishes my writer's heart and buoys my philosopher's soul because it holds more clues to the truth. Embracing complexity—the reality that we, our language, our behavior, our thoughts, are not easily defined or judged—is one of the best tools we have for leaning into compassion and repairing our interpersonal and societal relationships. If we neglect to investigate our beliefs, then misbeliefs may continue to shape our interactions.

## Compassion

Early on in my study of philosophy, a visiting professor offered my classmates and me an analogy for social inequities: Imagine that discrimination is a crease in a sheet of paper. To heal the crease, it is not enough to flatten it. Instead, we must first fold it in the other direction. In other words, equal treatment cannot undo past discrimination. Redress is needed to restore balance.

Her demonstration — with an actual sheet of paper — stuck with me. Affirmative action, DEI initiatives, news coverage that spotlights underrepresented communities, awards that limit eligibility to marginalized groups — these are attempts to heal historical wrongs by reversing the attention. So, too, is conscious language. Whenever we update our terminology, prioritize first-hand narratives, and seek diverse voices, we can acknowledge the enduring effects of exclusion that seep from one generation to the next.

It may surprise you to know that objectionable, questionable, offensive, insensitive, or inappropriate words are not automatically candidates for revamping. Someone posted on social media that they were accused of racism after using the term *Greek chorus*. But is it racist? A Greek chorus is a theatrical device, but time-honored traditions are not automatically excused. The deciding factor here is that this term does not demean any marginalized group or further their oppression, at least not in this context. Simply referring to race or ethnicity is not racist.

In theory, alternatives are not necessary if those who are directly affected by the use of a certain word do not perceive it as harmful. Sometimes insensitive language is simply that — insensitive without being oppressive. The ability to discern run-of-the-mill rudeness or insensitivity from language that harms a marginalized group (in a given context) will help you prioritize your limited time and energy. Ask: *Whose freedoms are being taken away? Whose oppression does this perpetuate?* However, if enough people believe that an innocuous word or phrase is offensive, then you may choose to avoid it regardless of whether it offends the affected communities.

To be clear, compassion is the desire to relieve suffering or distress, but it is not necessarily about emotion. Injustice fills me with productive anger, but the primary center of compassion is my reasoning brain, not my metaphoric heart. As a teen, I stopped eating meat because I wanted to choose a lesser harm, not because I was an animal lover. (I am not.) Today, my interest in conscious language arises from the desire to expose the power dynamics that preserve social inequities, not because I have great love for humankind. (I do not.) The danger of taking cues from our emotions is that emotions may be too fragile a foundation for a life-long practice. Our support of feminism, same-sex marriage, and the Black Lives Matter movement needs a plan of action. Therefore, my compassion is more *compass* than *passion*. When we have a stronger understanding of how the past shapes our thoughts, language, and interactions in the present, we can use language with more skill and contribute to healing, beginning with ourselves and those around us.

The presence of all five components is what makes language conscious: skillful selection of content, awareness of context, consideration of consequence, preservation of complexity, and emphasis on compassion. Pointing to a word or sentence or story and asking *Is this conscious language?* is really asking *Did the communicator consider the five Cs?* Let the five Cs help you maintain your focus on equity and liberation.

## *Key Points*

- Conscious language is language that promotes equity and freedom. To do so, it must be rooted in critical thinking and compassion, used skillfully in a specific context.
- Conscious language affirms our humanity and individuality and makes room for more of us to thrive.
- Using language consciously requires pausing to reflect before we act.
- Words have power, which means we have power. We all have a say in the shape and direction of language.

CONTENT

- Content is the most concrete part of communication, whereas context continually changes.
- We can use language to shift people's perceptions and create positive or negative changes.
- Words can come to mean different things to different people, because we imbue them with our own experiences.
- As individuals, we cannot control the ocean of language, but we can learn to navigate the waters.
- In general, skillful content involves clarifying our goals, knowing our audience, and manipulating other facets, including level of formality, persona, and tone.
- Ideally, our intended audience is based on potential—the true common denominator—not our biases of who should be included or excluded.

- Whenever we need to communicate with greater care, these content tools can help us choose an appropriate style for our message.

## CONTEXT

- Everything is context, and context is everything.
- The meaning of a word is influenced by the words, society, and history that surround it.
- Without context — a point of reference — words are meaningless.
- Content and context work together. Changing the context can change the meaning of content and vice versa.
- By consulting and adjusting context, we can more efficiently align impact with intention.
- Because context matters, no word is inherently harmful or healing.
- We can develop context that supports sensitive content, but some content may be unsalvageable.
- Context can be simplified as "people, past, present." *People* refers to the source and the receiver. *Past* refers to history and other patterns. *Present* refers to the circumstances, such as delivery method, length, timing, point of view, and surrounding words.
- The biggest variable is the audience. We cannot know what assumptions and associations each person brings to each word.
- Honing our everyday contextual awareness will help us promote inclusivity, respect, and empowerment.

CONSEQUENCE

- Unintentional discrimination is discrimination.
- Impact can override intention, so good intentions are not enough.
- Understanding common reactions to words and selecting them for impact is what storytellers do. These techniques can be used to emphasize humanity and encourage harmony.
- The impact of exclusionary language and other non-conscious language is the perpetuation of oppression, including negative mental and physical health consequences; lack of access to housing, healthcare, education, and employment; lack of federal funding, support, and services; biased laws and policies; ideologies of hate; abuse; murder; and genocide.
- Dehumanizing language is a known precursor to genocide.
- By using language that includes, confers respect, and self-empowers, we have the power to shift entrenched attitudes, especially our own.

COMPLEXITY

- Language that appears non-conscious may, surprisingly, be used to promote equity.
- Language can do harm and good in the same instance, because both concepts are relative and mutable, not binary. The most conscious option, therefore, may be language that does less harm, not no harm.
- Sorting language into dos and don'ts is unsustainable in

the long run. An ideal approach respects the gray areas and flexes with the context.

- Rules devoid of nuance are a hallmark of zero-tolerance policies.
- Recognizing complexity is crucial to healing the rifts in our society. It is one of the best tools we have for leaning into compassion and repairing relationships.

COMPASSION

- Equal treatment cannot undo past discrimination. Redress is needed to restore balance and can include updating our terminology, prioritizing firsthand narratives, and seeking diverse voices.
- Discerning between oppressive language and language that is offensive but not oppressive will help us focus on compassion.
- To determine whether language is perceived as harmful, we need to defer to those directly affected by it.
- If enough people outside of the affected group perceive a word as offensive, then you may choose to avoid it.
- Compassion, the desire to relieve suffering, is nothing without a plan of action.

The presence of all five Cs is what makes language conscious: skillful selection of content, awareness of context, consideration of consequence, preservation of complexity, and emphasis on compassion.

## Who Uses Conscious Language?

Chances are, *you* do.

Conscious language is simply an extension of everyday mindfulness. You may be conscious of your self-labels—a survivor who prefers the word *victim*, a Mexican American who identifies more as *Chicanx*, a nonbinary person who uses *he/him* pronouns. You may prefer to inform a friend privately of an unintentionally racist remark but confront a billion-dollar corporation publicly for the same language, taking power and responsibility into account. You may be conscious of listening and observing when your perspectives are overrepresented and speaking only to amplify a historically excluded voice. Many of us adapt to each situation instead of giving cookie-cutter responses. That is everyday conscious language.

Conscious language is necessary in most professional interactions. I have often observed how much kinder people are to coworkers than they are to their own families, where there is no shared expectation of respectful language. Unlike some, I do not mind the blame-y "Per my last email" or the pressuring "Thanks in advance," because it is conscious and considerate language for a subculture that expects a degree of performance in order to tolerate working together.

News outlets in general tend to invest in optimizing their use of conscious language, whether it is due to the weight of their responsibility to uphold accuracy, a desire for long-term viability, avoidance of mass criticism, or a bit of all three. Their behind-the-scenes grappling with conscious language is sometimes publicized in satisfyingly transparent explanations of style changes, such as *The New York Times'* "Why We're Capitalizing Black." In this nearly thousand-word piece, culture desk reporter Nancy Coleman begins with the past—W. E. B. Du Bois's eventually successful campaign to convince the *Times* to capitalize *Negro*—before introducing the recent decision to capitalize *Black* when referring to race.[13]

In addition to journalism, other spaces that care deeply about the impact of language include, no surprise, those whose success and efficacy hinge on their ability to serve the public: education, publishing, medicine, science, technology, business, public relations, advertising, marketing, publicity, philanthropy, arts, human resources, government, and religion.

Not wanting to appear outdated is a common reason to use language consciously. My 2004 copy of *The Christian Writer's Manual of Style* says, "When *He* is capped for God or Jesus, it can appear to younger readers especially, as though the author is purposely emphasizing the maleness of the deity, in direct response to feminist theologians who argue for the inclusiveness of God . . . The capitalized deity pronoun introduces a polemical overtone that may wholly detract from the topic at hand."[14]

Reading through style guides is one way I keep tabs on what matters to writers and editors. Many institutions maintain field-specific guidelines for gender-neutral terminology, writing about disability, inclusive language, and words to avoid. I know this because they frequently credit and link to ConsciousStyleGuide

.com, which is how I find them. (Thank you, NASA!) Because more people are using it, conscious language is catching on. And because conscious language is catching on, more people are using it.

### *Key Points*

- Conscious language is an extension of everyday mindfulness.
- Conscious language is used in all types of interactions, such as personal, professional, and social.
- People tend to use language consciously when they care about its impact, including how they appear to others.
- Many style guides provide suggestions for careful and purposeful language, an old concept.
- We spread conscious language by using it.

## When Do We Use Conscious Language?

Words and narratives about people take on heightened importance precisely because they are about people. Stray words that do not matter in discourse about places and things may unintentionally injure when people enter the picture. When we call fruit *ugly*, we are not oppressing fruit or the eaters of fruit. But applying that word to babies or other humans or even nonhuman animals may unintentionally promote prejudice and discrimination.

Every person has their own sensitivities about language, whether it is mundane grammatical peeving, a personal nerve about a particular word, or feeling threatened by an unfair characterization. Careful and compassionate language cannot reconcile unknowable personal traumas, but it is one tool we can develop to help us express ourselves better and be understood.

We can use conscious language when we want to:

- be clear
- be fair
- be accurate
- be specific
- be descriptive
- tell our own stories
- tell other people's stories
- avoid causing distress
- express compassion
- shift perspectives
- change the status quo
- include
- respect
- empower

In short, conscious language can be used whenever we want to be more aware, mindful, and intentional with communication. When do you want to lean into thoughtfulness? That's when you can use conscious language.

THE CONSCIOUS STYLE GUIDE

*Key Points*
---

- Language about people is important precisely because it is about people and can unintentionally cause harm.
- Even though we cannot predict the impact of language with any certainty, we can use conscious language to express ourselves and be understood.
- Conscious language helps us be clear, fair, and accurate so we can tell our own stories and those of others with compassion.
- Whenever we want to be more aware, mindful, and intentional with communication, we can use conscious language.

## What Conscious Language Is Not

To understand what conscious language is, it may help to know what it is not.

**Conscious language is not political correctness.** Politically correct language is about using terms intended to avoid offense. From the outside, conscious language may look and feel like PC language, but when we treat conscious language like a phrase book instead of a contextual tool, it is no longer conscious. PC language treats words as "one size fits all," whereas conscious language favors flexibility and complexity. PC language is often adopted due to fear of criticism, whereas conscious language often arises from compassion.

Conscious language is more than replacing nouns and

pronouns. Without question, conscious language is about words, but words working with context. Operating solely at the word level, as PC language does, means too many choices about context — the words surrounding the word — will have already been made. It is challenging to make a deep impact with shallow changes. This is why conscious language is rooted in equity and not in being "correct."

**Conscious language does not always include everyone.** When we encounter exclusionary language, a typical response would be to use a less biased option, like replacing *mankind* with *humankind* and *boys and girls* with *children* to include all genders/ sexes. But practicing conscious language does not mean stripping all social attributes from language. It is about examining how words, representations, and narratives prejudge. Sometimes prejudices persist because language is not exclusive enough, like saying *communities of color* when the issues are specific to Black communities. Or referring to men's sports as *sports* while referring to women's sports as *women's sports*. When terminology lacks the necessary specificity, the issue becomes one of factual accuracy, not just politics or fairness.

So conscious language is not about including everyone all the time or "rounding up" from specific terms to umbrella terms. It is OK to keep our spotlight narrow and precise. Promoting equity requires the exclusion of overrepresented or frequently represented groups so we can center less visible groups and raise awareness about issues and experiences specific to them.

**Conscious language is not niceness or inoffensiveness.** Being offended and feeling discomfort may be false gauges of whether a piece of content liberates or limits. If equity is the goal, then the question is whether offending will have equitable impacts. Offending people is a risk I willingly take with every talk I give, every article and book I write.

If niceness is your North Star, then what if conscious language itself offends? A trans woman's *she/her* pronouns may offend an anti-trans professor. A Jewish sensitivity reader's flagging of antisemitic portrayals may offend the writer. A disabled patron's request for a straw at dining establishments may offend environmentalists with zero tolerance for single-use plastics. Being nice is nice, but language for liberation is not about making people comfortable.

Naming invisible norms may be offensive to members of a dominant culture who are accustomed to the luxury of not being named. Should we avoid the potential offense of terms like *White*, *cisgender*,[*] and *allopathic*?[†] Moratoriums against offensive language can discourage us from using words as tools. You might not care for the word *penis* popping up unexpectedly (sorry), but teaching children the names of body parts helps them discourage potential perpetrators, take ownership of their bodies, and communicate clearly when asking for help. You may be hearing *clitoris* from the mouths of babes, but the alternative—not

---

[*]The coining of *cisgender* is credited to Dana Defosse, a retired researcher and physician educator, while she was a graduate student in 1994, according to her article for *HuffPost*, "I Coined the Term 'Cisgender' 29 Years Ago. Here's What This Controversial Word Really Means" (February 18, 2023).

[†]*Allopathic* describes medicine, surgery, radiation, and other conventional treatments as opposed to alternative medicine.

familiarizing children with these terms—has stronger potential for harm.

If conscious language ran parallel with anti-offensive language, then practitioners of conscious language should question *butt* or *ass* when *bottom* or *fanny* will do. (Uh-oh, you know that *fanny* means "vulva" in the UK, right?) To what end will we be trying to prevent the unpreventable? What offends is too arbitrary and temporary and contextual to be an enemy of conscious language. Better we direct our energy toward making space than making nice.

This raises the question: What is "offensive language," really? Calling stereotypes, harmful narratives, misrepresentation, and other exclusionary language "offensive" can turn a fight for equity into a complaint about hurt feelings. Biased language may interfere with mental health, ability to work, right to marry, freedom to be ourselves—all facets of our lives. When language has the power to take from us our liberties and protections, calling it "offensive" reduces it to a personal problem instead of a systemic failure.

Conscious language can be anarchic in its flexibility and not at all nice when the situation calls for steely bluntness. The reality is that stark language can wake people up. Calls for civility when marginalized groups are rising up and speaking out against injustice is oftentimes about control, not conversation. To make strides in equity, communicating consciously may call for harsh language if not stronger actions, such as protests and boycotts. Nice language doesn't cut it when it allows existing power structures to stay intact. Using language that is aware, mindful, and intentional includes taking the most direct path and saying it like it is.

### Key Points

- Conscious language is not political correctness. Though they overlap, conscious language values context, flexibility, complexity, and compassion and addresses language beyond nouns and pronouns. The driver of conscious language is equity, not being "correct."
- Conscious language does not always include everyone. Rather than automatically resorting to broad language, using language consciously means naming specific groups and addressing their specific issues to raise visibility and awareness.
- Conscious language is not niceness or inoffensiveness. Instead of judging language by its offensiveness, judge it for its potential to liberate. When nice and civil language allows existing power structures to stay intact, we can achieve more by using stark language.

## Limitations

Conscious language is not a magic scepter that shoots out beams of beautiful wokeness that erase centuries of injustice. Nor is it an invisible shield that renders us impervious to criticism. Speaking and writing consciously requires practice, patience, all-around forgiveness, and a pinch of cynicism. So before you get into the folds and contours of your own practice, I want to discuss some limitations of conscious language to hedge your expectations.

**Neutrality is relative.** The word *neutral* is evoked often in discussions of conscious language. It touts freedom from bias, judgment, and opinion, a state of neither this nor that, like *gender-neutral*. But is neutral language truly neutral? Neutrality is not a discrete point but degrees on a scale. *Gender-neutral* implies a midpoint on some gender-measuring scale, making its meaning dependent on the gender binary. *Gender-free*, in contrast, is free of gender.

The myth of neutrality can be observed in the following examples. Take the synonyms *cat*, *feline*, *kitty*, and *pussy*. Objectively, they are free of bias, judgment, and opinion. However, our personal and collective associations—as part of the context—make them less than neutral.

Anticipating audience bias is necessary when anticipating consequence. "Neutral" medical terms, like *geriatric* and *obese*, can easily become pejorative, which affects a patient's quality of care and ability to improve their health. "Neutral" words can have racist or sexist or disablist overtones in questionable contexts, like patronizingly referring to Black people as *articulate*, stereotyping Latinas as *spicy*, or presuming that all chronically ill people are *struggling*. Bias adds shade to neutral words over time through repeated associations, like applying *bossy* to assertive girls and women more often than to assertive boys and men. Biases, fortunately, can also fade through association, like the increasingly gender-free *dude*, which is going the way I had hoped *guy* would go. Neutral language is a necessary goal, but words by themselves have no inherent neutrality. Words can only be made more or less neutral by context.

**Language evolution is unpredictable.** Psst...everything will change. Trying to predict which words will gain or lose popularity due to their associations may be futile. For instance, it would be premature for us to jump the gun and obliterate common phrases like *jump the gun* in anticipation of offense (origin: track races). Once a term gains or loses a critical mass of supporters, then we can assess its contextual usefulness through our framework. All the more reason to learn how to apologize, forgive, and navigate perceived transgressions with grace. But until then, let's give more attention to addressing known harms instead of sound-alikes and feel-alikes.

**Bias is not malice.** It may be tempting to prejudge someone by the words they use, but doing so reveals more about our biases than theirs. There is a chasm of difference between people who don't use conscious language and people hostile to equity or the idea of personal responsibility. Also, action is not attitude, behavior is not belief. Mainstream adoption of equitable language is not evidence that our society's deepest prejudices have eased. Only that the linguistic consensus has shifted. Use of exclusionary language does not expose the bigotry of the user, because misalignment between attitude and action happens to the most dedicated of advocates, including yours truly. (For more on this topic, see chapter four's "Understanding Misalignment" on page 193.)

**Impacts change over time.** Does replacing outdated content in classics erase evidence of oppression? Does disinviting controversial speakers erode free speech? Does firing instructors for unpopular stances make academia hostile to both learning and teaching? Linguistic impacts are not always clear. Short-term benefits may become long-term harms, and short-term harms may become long-term benefits. Having patience allows us to experiment, refrain from quick judgment, and thrive in the face of predictable but temporary chaos.

**Sometimes, no word is adequate.** Umbrella terms may simultaneously be useful and wholly inadequate. They have collective power, but if *people of color* essentially means "everybody but White people" and *LGBTQIA+* essentially means "everybody but straight cis people," then why avoid saying the latter? I like to dip into my quota of *non-* prefixes (you get a limited supply when you join the conscious language community) and use *non-White* and *non-straight* on occasion for clarity and simplicity. Many of my peers would knit their brows at that, because *non-* constructions center the group mentioned. In this case, it centers White people and straight people, two groups in the US with more privilege. But if that's the logic, then what about the preferred terms *asexual, agender, atheist,* and *gender nonconforming*, which emphasize *-sexual, -gender, -theist,* and *-conforming*? When conscious language gets tricky, it is more important to be flexible than consistent.

**Conscious language is not the destination.** It is a beginning. Or a practice in tandem with direct action. So write to your representatives, give proper attribution to marginalized people, diversify your staff and sources, fund marginalized artists and organizations, march and write and speak in protest, and invest your time and energy in other conscious actions that challenge and repair inequitable systemic beliefs and practices.

### *Key Points*

- Neutrality is relative. Words can be made more or less neutral only by context.
- Language evolution is unpredictable. Better to prioritize known harms than try to predict the changes to come.
- Bias is not malice. There's a big difference between people who use biased language and people who are hostile to equity. Misalignment happens.
- Impacts change over time. Short-term benefits may become long-term harms, and short-term harms may become long-term benefits.
- Sometimes, no word is adequate. When conscious language gets tricky, it is more important to be flexible than consistent.
- Conscious language is not the destination. It is one of many conscious actions that can challenge and repair inequity.

## CHAPTER TWO

# PLAN

An ideal conscious language practice is one that creates more ease and calm in your life while maximizing your ability to do good. When you make it a habit to observe your mind, try on new perspectives, question your assumptions, and notice the language around you, every moment becomes an opportunity to build confidence.

In this chapter, I lead you through some self-inquiry and self-reflection. This part of the framework is about understanding how you think so that you can develop a practice that grows with you. Clarifying your interests, intentions, and boundaries will help you process language issues more objectively and maintain your course.

The first thing to know about your mind is that your assumptions are often beyond your control. So to set the stage for thinking about thinking, let's discuss ways we can detect and counter implicit biases.

## Disrupting Implicit Biases

Implicit biases are invisible attitudes about the world that form without our consent. Also known as *unconscious biases*, they underlie our cogitation, distort our perceptions, skew our judgment, and pervade our behaviors. Just by going about our lives, we can spread implicit biases by communicating our pleasure and displeasure through words, tone of voice, facial expression, gestures, and body language.

Mass media—including books, newspapers, film, television, and the internet—is often the first blamed for amplifying biases. But behind every program, platform, presentation, and algorithm are faces. Behind every piece of content uttered or written or produced is a decision-maker. And with the proliferation of personal websites, blogs, podcasts, and social media, individuals have become the media. The media is us. Rather than looking away and pointing fingers at the abstract but omnipotent "media" behind the curtains, we can look for the humans and foment a rebellion one person at a time. As individuals, we may not be in control of the misrepresentations that flood our unconscious minds, but we can use conscious language to voice our dissent, interrogate our biases, and disintegrate injurious narratives.

Detecting bias is tricky, because we tend to confuse our initial reaction with insight: *I am scared of that person; therefore, they must be scary.* But gut reactions are not an objective gauge, because the dots were preconnected for us. Language that repeatedly associates certain groups with disgust, distrust, and inferiority primes us to autocomplete these equations on our own. Who is smarter, safer, more relatable, more reliable? Who is better suited to rent, work, lead, win? Though they feel like truth, gut instincts are more likely the product of a lifetime of messages and impressions.

We may not be able to control our first reaction, but we can work on changing our subsequent reactions. Being sensitive to the workings of implicit bias upon our thoughts, beliefs, and behaviors is the first step to disrupting knee-jerk conclusions. If we pause to observe our initial reactions, then we may be able to learn something about ourselves and why we think what we think. *I am scared of that person. But...they are not doing anything scary. Isn't it interesting how I am reacting to their race/gender/age/appearance?* Our first thoughts do not represent us unless our subsequent thoughts do not change.

Another hint that implicit bias is at work is the prejudgment of customs and behaviors as "normal" or "not normal" despite obvious similarities. Like excluding housework from the category of *real work*. Or calling North Korea's wake-up song *creepy* but the Christianity-promoting Pledge of Allegiance *patriotic*. Or decrying China's human rights abuses while ignoring the United States' own. Biases also mask other cognitive incongruences. We kill pigs for ham and bacon though they are smarter than human toddlers. We scorn violence but casually smack men because "they can take it." We comprehend the cycle of intergenerational poverty but find ourselves blaming people for being poor.

The good news is that, according to the Kirwan Institute for the Study of Race and Ethnicity, implicit biases can be unlearned.[1] I propose that we begin by increasing our alertness to bias activation. Taking an instant dislike to someone, believing in such a thing as "common sense," jumping to conclusions after reading a headline, underexplaining something because "everybody knows this," ascribing personal preferences to a social attribute (*I like pink because I'm a girl*)—these and other everyday reactions can be tip-offs that underlying attitudes are limiting our thoughts. Once we become attuned to potential leaps in logic, then we can ask ourselves one simple question: *Why do I believe this?* By meeting potential bias with patient self-inquiry, we may be able to prevent ourselves from slipping into the same well-worn grooves from reaction to conclusion.

### *Key Points*

- Implicit biases are invisible attitudes about the world that form without our consent. They affect everything we think and do, and we spread these biases as we go about our lives.
- Biases are amplified through mass media, which includes websites, blogs, podcasts, and social media.
- We may not be able to control our initial reactions, but we can work on changing our subsequent reactions.
- Implicit biases can be unlearned.
- We can be alert to signs of bias activation by noticing our assumptions and asking, *Why do I believe this?*

## Shifting Your Perspective

When I was a teen, I developed a habit of mentally swapping out people's physical and social attributes, which I called *cycling*. By imagining them with a different gender/sex, race, age, or appearance, I could observe my implicit biases lurching into the foreground. It was not flattering to repeatedly confirm what a jerk I am. But the exercise was illuminating, allowing me to recognize and counter my patterns of resistance.

Cycling can be used in many ways. You can compare the impact of tone or terminology by cycling identifiers. Do you perceive a difference between *Blacks* and *the Blacks*? Would you say *Whites* or *the Whites*? The inappropriateness of certain terms and phrases — like *the Blacks, the Chinese, the gays* — can become more obvious through comparison. You can check for bias in narrative and description. Would you describe a man as a parent first, like women often are? Would you describe a boy as *nurturing* or a girl as *risk-taking*? Would you say an American-born White person is *Americanized* or use the word only with non-White Americans? Would you think of a sexually interested younger man or older woman as *dirty*, an adjective often applied to older men? You can spot uneven treatment when giving praise or credit. Are you less likely to acknowledge people behind the scenes? Are you more likely to use the work, ideas, and intellectual property of members of a marginalized group without attribution or permission?

Cycling can be used for purposes other than bias detection. It can increase awareness of power and privilege or their absence. As a fiction writer, I use cycling for character development. Bringing fictional people to life in a contemporary tale may require an understanding of each character's intersecting identities, cultures, and subcultures. Cycling can reveal the influence of power — past and present — in ways that throw social inequities into sharp relief. How does cycling sexual orientation, marital status, or socioeconomic background change the pressures your character must deal with? Being sensitive to how history affects the characters in your story can help you subvert or avoid stereotypes, clichéd portrayals, and other widely held misbeliefs.

Lastly, you can cycle yourself. This is known as "putting yourself in someone else's shoes." Imagining another's experience can spark our compassion and sense of injustice. Here are a few scenarios:

- Imagine having to endure baby talk from strangers because they think you are old.
- Imagine undergoing treatment for drug use and a health-care practitioner calling you a *junkie*.
- Imagine trying to watch a film as a blind person, but your local theaters do not offer audio description.
- Imagine being excluded from meetings, not because of the quality of your work but because you are trans.
- Imagine being told that your manuscript about your racially marginalized culture "won't sell," while publishers acquire poorly researched stories by White writers about your culture.
- Imagine taking your child to the park and someone calling the cops on you because you are a man.
- Imagine having served time for a crime and not being able to shed the label of *convict* during job searches.
- Imagine having dark skin when *dark* and *darkness* are common metaphors for malevolence, negativity, and emptiness.

- Imagine having schizophrenia and rarely encountering a realistic portrayal of it in the media.
- Imagine being a child who sees people of their own ethnicity in picture books portrayed only as ugly caricatures or in colors that don't look human.
- Imagine a journalist asking about your breasts or butt because you are a woman, your genitalia because you are trans, or whether you are a top or a bottom because you are gay.

Adopting another perspective can be humbling, but remember, cycling may not always be effective and it will not replace lived experience. What it can do is expand your awareness.

### *Key Points*

- In order to observe signs of implicit biases within ourselves and notice differences in how we perceive and treat people, we can use our imaginations to "cycle" someone's characteristics, identifiers in descriptions, or the people in a given situation.
- Cycling can help expand our awareness, but it may not be effective and does not replace lived experience.

## Knowing Yourself

To build a sustainable and scalable framework for conscious language, get to know your primary tool—yourself. By understanding how you learn, how you adapt, and what you value, you can flex and grow within and past the boundaries that you set.

## Identifying Your Motivations

Why do you want to learn conscious language? There is no wrong answer. Maybe you want to learn conscious language because it is expected at your job. Maybe you want to be aware of the potential impact of your words. Maybe you want to know what the fuss is about. Phrased another way: What brings you to conscious language? What does using conscious language mean in your life? Why are you reading this book?

Take a few minutes to make a note of your motivations. Here are a few to get you started. Perhaps...

1. You are curious about conscious language. You want more word choices and options for communication. You want to boost your cultural literacy. You want to deepen your appreciation for context.

2. You want to build trust. You want to be understood. You want to be tactful and respectful. You want to coexist with a wide range of people. You want to use language that is aligned with your beliefs.

3. You want to alleviate suffering. You want to promote the well-being of others. You want to treat people the way they want to be treated. You want to be more aware of how power and privilege influence interactions.

4.  You want to connect with a more relevant audience. You want to be conscious of your language on your platform. You want to distinguish yourself from competitors. You want to be considerate of your audience's concerns.

Number one is about self-improvement (personal). Number two is about creating meaningful connections (social). Number three is about responsibility and repair (ethical). And number four is about brand and business excellence (professional). Most of us will identify with more than one reason. If you are a healthcare practitioner, for example, conscious language can help you develop an attentive and nonjudgmental bedside manner to improve patient health, which combines personal, social, ethical, and professional aspects. Understanding your specific motivations will help you stay on track and move toward your goals.

## Exploring Your Interests

Conscious language spans all language that has an impact on people, animals, our climate, and our planet. To avoid becoming overwhelmed, start with areas you are interested in and good at or things you can do easily. Refer to your motivations or the suggestions below on how to break down this vast subject. Purposely restricting your study of conscious language can be calming, particularly if too many options induce anxiety. So familiarize yourself in stages, the way you typically learn other things, like cooking, parenting, or recycling.

Here are some approaches to consider:

**Do you want to specialize?** What has your attention? You can specialize in a type, topic, audience, or style. Examples of types are accessibility, inclusive language, plain language. Examples of topics are food, science journals, Nigerian culture. Examples of audience are children, patients, LGBTQIA+ communities. Examples of style are AP style, APA style, house style.

Or you can sharpen your focus. Within accessibility features, you can specialize in audio descriptions. Within food and dining, you can specialize in plant-based terminology. Within publishing, you can specialize in conscious style in children's books. Within inclusive language, you can specialize in cultural consultation.

Or ask yourself what will help create more ease in your life. If your job requires you to write job descriptions, you can learn how gendered assumptions are expressed through language. To host a sangha or other spiritual group, you can practice words of welcome and reassurance. To comfort a friend with cancer, you can follow their lead in using or avoiding "battle" and "fight" metaphors. Start with one meaningful aspect and then allow your interests to grow organically.

**Do you want to triage?** What areas have the most urgency? Triaging is prioritizing by need. With conscious language, triaging can look like prioritizing actions with the highest impacts; prioritizing actions related to terms, descriptions, and narratives widely known to be harmful; or prioritizing actions that lead to institutional or wide-scale change. Triaging helps you manage your limited time and energy efficiently.

One type of triaging is reducing the frequency of inappropriate language instead of avoiding it completely. Having do-mores and do-lesses instead of dos and don'ts is more realistic when you are getting accustomed to using conscious language.

Many of us may end up triaging, not by intention but by default. Being a conscious language jack-of-all-trades requires an enormous expenditure of time. Even with the help of artificial intelligence and technology, there's too much content for us to monitor, consume, analyze, process, document, and retain in a meaningful way. So take a deep breath. Prioritizing can help you excel.

**Do you want to lead?** What can you do with your power and influence? If you can influence the way people think and behave, impact the distribution of resources and opportunities, or control access to what people need to live and thrive, then you have the ability and the responsibility to effect higher-level change. There is an expectation for people with power to take proportionate action, because lack of action will be interpreted as condoning the status quo. So if you are part of a collective, a company, a nonprofit, or a government that can lead others in using language more consciously, then consider expanding your scope to match or surpass your level of responsibility.

By leading, you can inspire others to take action. As individuals, many of us hold gatekeeping roles — editors, teachers, caretakers, librarians, social media users, entrepreneurs — that give us varying degrees of influence over the spread of language. In some circles, gatekeeping means not letting people through, but we gatekeepers can be gate openers. And as gate openers, we can let through more of the voices, ideas, and identities we want to nurture and protect.

To be clear, leading does not mean calling out your peers on social media, banning books with outdated language, or any action that discourages critical thought and discussion. Leading is passing the mic around, modeling respectful communication, and establishing policies that reflect and welcome the diversity of humankind. People who are part of a dominant culture are in a stronger position to use their influence, access, and connections to boost people of marginalized cultures. Leading is opening the gate to acceptance.

If you need more clarity on your approach, I invite you to delve into the resources on ConsciousStyleGuide.com and take note of what interests you. If your motivation for learning conscious language is related to duty — to family, faith, work, or society — then let that draw the map. For the sake of your longevity as a conscious language user, consider starting with boundaries you can manage, and expand them as you go.

## Thinking Critically

When you learn that a word or description or narrative has been called into question, use the five Cs to help you process the information. Some questions you can ask:

- **Content:** *Is the language skillful in itself?*
- **Context:** *Is the language appropriate for the context?*

- **Consequence:** *Are the anticipated consequences of the language acceptable?*
- **Complexity:** *Does the language acknowledge nuance and complexity?*
- **Compassion:** *Does the language promote equity or freedom?*

If the five Cs have been satisfied, then the issue may not be worthy of our attention. (Think *Greek chorus.*) If one or multiple areas are deficient, you can use the five Cs as a checklist for developing more conscious language.

Because people tend to disagree on which potential harms to prioritize or acknowledge, we can further investigate the situation—and our conscious philosophies—by asking ourselves questions such as:

- *Who or what is the source of the claim? Are they part of the affected group? How many are making the claim?*
- *If the credibility of the source is unknown, what do credible sources (if any) advise?*
- *What are the arguments for using or avoiding certain language? What are the common practices for comparable contexts?*
- *Will the audience understand the alternatives? What type of bridge (meaning additional context) will aid comprehension?*
- *What are the potential short-term and long-term consequences of continuing to use certain language or of using alternatives? Can negative consequences be avoided or mitigated by changing the context to support the language?*

Over time, you may notice that the issues that emerge tend to fall under certain types. By familiarizing yourself with types of potentially non-conscious language, you can decide on a course of action more quickly. (Chapter three's "Zoom Levels," on page 80, covers many broad types to watch out for.) To aid your self-exploration, I present below some types of language that people tend to find challenging or highly debatable.

In discussing specific words and phrases within these types, my intention is to illuminate the process of evaluating, not to shape your conclusions about their use. Sometimes the mere mention of a word as possibly inappropriate may cause people to recoil from said word regardless of context. I hope that my pointing this out helps you be more aware of how your mind works and the reactions these words may provoke. How you respond to these types of words—and how flexible your boundaries are—can provide clues to an approach that you can sustain and scale. At the end of this section are some suggestions for action that can further reveal your preferences.

**Do you use words with troubling origins?** Before *cakewalk* meant "easy task," it referred to a dance created by enslaved people of African descent to mock White people. *Tipping point* means a critical juncture for drastic change, but up till the 1990s, according to *Merriam-Webster*, it was "a precursor of sorts to the phenomenon of *white flight*"—White families moving out of a neighborhood after Black families moved in. Saying that someone has *gone off the reservation*, meaning "deviated in an unexpected way," invokes a history of the US government literally restricting Native peoples to reservations.

These are examples of common phrases, still in use, that some advocates of conscious language avoid because of their racial or racist origins. Other advocates would say that avoidance should be based on whether the groups directly affected by the words find them harmful. Regarding the examples above, Native communities unambiguously discourage the metaphorical use of *off the reservation*. But it is unclear whether Black communities consider *cakewalk* or *tipping point* harmful. (The National Association of Black Journalists style guide, last updated in October 2022, does not cover these terms.) Would you avoid *cakewalk* and *tipping point*?

The word *brainstorm* has been discussed for years as potentially harmful to people with epilepsy. It originally meant a "fit of acute delirious mania," according to Online Etymology Dictionary. But a 2015 survey of people with epilepsy by the Epilepsy Society showed overwhelmingly that *brainstorm* is not considered offensive when used in the context of a group gathering ideas. Additionally, "some people even felt more offended when people substituted the term 'brainstorming' [with] another term so as to not cause offence."[2] Knowing that some people outside of these communities consider *brainstorm* offensive, would you avoid *brainstorm* when referring to idea-gathering?

If you were to avoid everyday words based on troubling origins, it may lead to inconsistent actions. If we avoid *cakewalk* for its racial beginnings, should we then eschew ragtime music, which originated from cakewalks? Also, a bigger deal tends to be made of origins that are potentially racist, but what about other types of biases? If you oppose religious oppression, would you avoid saying *goodbye*? It was derived from a contraction of *God be with ye*. If you oppose violent language, would you avoid *deadline*? It referred to a drawn boundary at a prison that, if crossed by prisoners, exposed them to getting shot. If you oppose sexism, would you nix the word *hysteria*? It originally referred to a mental health condition thought to be caused by a wandering uterus. Would you use any of these terms?

**Do you use words rumored to have troubling origins?** Articles about word origins are helpful in my line of work—except when they are untrue. A recent dive into such words and phrases revealed the lack of evidence against them.

*Picnic* is frequently listed among words with racist origins, suspected of having etymological ties to lynching. But according to the Reuters Fact Check team, this rumor is false.[3] The association may have come about because "lynching picnics,"[4] attended by White men, women, and children, were picnic-like gatherings at which someone, usually an African American man, was killed.

*Basket case* was rumored to refer to badly injured soldiers. But there is "no evidence that any head-and-torso survivors from any country were carried around in baskets," says *Grammarphobia*.[5] Still, you may want to exercise caution with its common meaning, "emotionally disturbed" or "unable to cope."

*Long time no see* is a word-for-word translation of the Mandarin phrase *hao jiu bu jian*. It is a benign and commonplace greeting that originated within early Chinese immigrant communities in the US. Some people nowadays claim that White settlers used this phrase to mock Native peoples, and therefore, it should be avoided.* If it is true that White people misappropriated *long time no see* for harm, this raises two issues: Should a dominant culture have the right to take over a marginalized culture's term? And should a dominant culture's misuse of a marginalized culture's term be allowed to taint it? People who advocate for protecting this and other phrases from misappropriation would say no and no.

In a similar case, place-names and business names that include the word *squaw* have been challenged because the *S*-word, as it is known in some circles, is believed to be a racist and sexual slur. But *squaw* is a phonetic rendering of an Algonkian word that means "the totality of being female," according to Margaret Bruchac, an associate professor of anthropology at the University of Pennsylvania. "Banning the word will not erase the past, and will only give the oppressors the power to define our language... If we accept the slander, and internalize the insult, we discredit our female ancestors who felt no shame at hearing the word spoken. To ban Indigenous words discriminates against Native people and their languages."[6] Would you avoid any of these words or phrases?

Note: The difficulty in ascertaining the truth can complicate good intentions. Though these examples hopefully vindicate words that have been wronged, other evidence may be uncovered in the future.

---

*Their edict may be partly based on the alternate origin story, that *long time no see* came from Native communities. But according to the *Oxford English Dictionary*, the etymology is Chinese, and the first citation, from 1892, referenced Chinese people. Mandarin speakers continue to use the original Mandarin greeting.

**Do you use offensive words in a non-offensive context?**
Some homonyms of offensive words have endured because they
are used in a specialized context. *Glory hole* is slang for a hole in a
wall used for anonymous, depersonalized sexual acts. But a *glory
hole* is also a hole in the side of a furnace used to soften glass.
*Chink* is a slur usually referring to a person of Chinese descent.
But in cabin building, *chinks* are log gaps that you fill in with
moss, stones, wood, or other materials, called *chinking*. *Cripple* is
a derogatory word referring to a person with a disabled limb. But
a *cripple wall* is a short wall in a section of a house designed to give
out during seismic activity. *Cripple wall* may be gradually falling
out of favor, with *pony wall*, its synonym, rising in popularity. But
*glory hole* and *chinking* are still popular in their fields, judging by
their use on national TV. When words share the same spelling
and pronunciation but have different meanings, the context helps
us determine which word is intended. But if one of the meanings
is perceived to cause harm, should we avoid the word in all contexts? Would you avoid the specialized use of *glory hole*, *chink*, or
*cripple wall*?

**Do you make a distinction between words for things and
words for people?** Words like *abnormal*, *deviant*, *Oriental*, *crazy*,
and *lazy* are considered derogatory. But some users of conscious
language consider them appropriate when the context is about
things and not people. Describing people as *abnormal* or *deviant*
stigmatizes. But *abnormal* can be safely applied to test results or
the weather, and *deviant* is neutral and useful in statistical analysis. The word *Oriental* stereotypes and exoticizes people of East
Asian or Middle Eastern descent. But when applied to things—

*Oriental medicine, Oriental rugs, Orientalwood,* and *oriental topaz* — the word is considered benign. Calling someone *crazy* dismisses their agency and conjures up false stereotypes of violent behavior. But when used to describe events, situations, and objects — *crazy line, crazy delicious, crazy about my kids* — it can be done mindfully.[7] Also, *crazy quilt, crazy golf,* and *crazy bone* are compound words that refer to specific things that are unrelated to mental illness. Accusing people of being *lazy* judges them based on their productivity and ignores possible issues with brain health, such as depression. But we can enjoy a *lazy nap,* pet a bunny's *lazy ears,* have a *lazy eye* (amblyopia), criticize a *lazy stereotype.* Would you avoid applying *abnormal, deviant, Oriental, crazy,* or *lazy* to things?

**Do you alternate between options or choose one?** People take different approaches when communities disagree on which identifier is more appropriate, such as identity-first language (*disabled person*) or person-first language (*person with a disability*). (For a detailed discussion, see "Types of Identifiers" on page 153.) Some use one term exclusively. Some use one term first and/or most. Some alternate. Mixing terms is something that the *Publication Manual of the American Psychological Association* (APA style) advises: "It is permissible to use either approach or to mix person-first and identity-first language unless or until you know that a group clearly prefers one approach... Mixing this language may help you avoid cumbersome repetition of 'person with...' and is also a means to change how authors and readers regard disability and people within particular disability communities."[8]

The more familiar someone is with the culture and

communities, the more creative and confident they can be with diverging from basic options. In *Dwell's* "Villages for Unhoused People Are Popping Up in More Cities. What's It Like to Live in Them?," journalist Hannah Wallace uses *people in need of housing, people were experiencing homelessness, people without a home, unsheltered people, unhoused individuals,* and *people with experience living without a home.*[9] Would you mix terms, choose one, or get creative?

These examples are neither conscious nor non-conscious. Thinking critically means that you determine your own conscious language style. For each, ask yourself if you lean toward a particular course of action. Namely, you could:

- **Use or avoid categorically.** For example, if you believe that any term with a harmful origin must be avoided, then you can replace all such terms by default. However, categorical rejection ignores the complexity of individual cases. Some claims about harmful origins may actually be misinformation, because origins are often muddled or unknowable.

- **Use or avoid depending on the source.** For example, if people claim that a term is racist, you can determine your course of action based on their authority. Identifying where claims of inappropriateness come from encourages discernment between sources and deferring to people with the relevant identity or experience. But how much support do you require when deciding whether to use or avoid the language in question? One voice? A group of voices? A

groundswell of voices? The actual number of credible supporters may be difficult to assess.

- **Use or avoid case by case.** For example, if contexts vary
  too greatly to establish an overarching guideline, you can
  assess the cases individually until you observe patterns in
  your style. The benefit of this approach is that it increases
  your familiarity with the specifics and deepens your
  knowledge. However, case-by-case assessment usually
  requires more time, energy, and research.

- **Avoid when in doubt.** For example, if you strive to do the
  least harm, you can immediately avoid or replace the language in question while you investigate claims of inappropriateness. Please note: Though this approach may initially
  avoid inadvertent harm, the alternatives themselves may
  be equally questionable.*

- **Wait and see.** For example, if it isn't clear how the groups
  directly impacted by the language feel about it, you can
  delay action while monitoring the situation. This, however, may encourage chronic inaction and avoidance.

Often, the ideal approach is decided by practicality: If you are
short on time, broad rules may make more sense than case-by-case
scrutiny. If you trust only current meanings and impacts, you
may choose to ignore rumored origins. If your choices are

---

*Upon learning that describing an Asian person's eyes as *slanted* is derogatory, an editor in an online forum decided to use *tilted* instead, trading one otherizing term for
another. (Tip: Instead of describing a marginalized person's features, which tends to
be from a Eurocentric perspective, consider identifying their race/ethnicity.)

constrained by red tape and external approvals, you may need to take a wait-and-see attitude for everything. By finding the patterns, you can address the underlying issues that help or hinder your progress.

## *Key Points*

### IDENTIFYING YOUR MOTIVATIONS

- Your motivations may be personal, social, ethical, or professional. Understanding your specific motivations will help you stay on track.

### EXPLORING YOUR INTERESTS

- Conscious language spans all language that has an impact on people, animals, our climate, and our planet. To avoid becoming overwhelmed, start with areas you are interested in and good at or things you can do easily.
- You can specialize in a type, topic, audience, or style that interests you.
- You can triage and prioritize actions to manage your time and energy.
- You can be a leader and open the gate, inspire action, and effect higher-level change.

### THINKING CRITICALLY

- The five Cs will help you identify problems with and remedies for language being questioned.
- You can investigate further by examining the source, their credibility, the arguments, the common practices, the

alternatives, the short- and long-term consequences, and possible mitigation through contextualization.
- Categorizing potentially non-conscious language by type and identifying patterns in your responses can help reveal your personal conscious style.

## Observing Actively

Our external and internal worlds are flush with hints about the optimal direction for our conscious language practice. But sometimes we are too preoccupied by the past or the future to use our mind and senses in the present. Through self-directed curiosity, we can slip into the meditative mode of active observation — gathering information while slowing the pace of judgment. Many answers to our questions about conscious language — which terms are popular, who uses what — can be gleaned by noticing what is already within and around us.

If you already practice a form of nonjudgmental observation, the tips below can help you be attentive to language in particular.

## The Outer World

External observation means reading attentively, listening deeply, and increasing our attunement to the use of language around us. Because language is alive, newer uses of conscious language cannot be found in books. Notice the mindfulness in the words around you. In particular, notice uses that affirm your own uses as well as uses that are new to you. The latter may be more inspiring and educational. To respect individual differences, avoid attributing language usage by one person to an entire group.

For an idea of what observations of conscious language are like, here are some of mine over the past few months.

- I noticed that in a survey, Panda Express had the options *Female, Male, Non-binary/third gender, Prefer to self-describe,* and *Prefer not to answer.*
- I noticed the term *skin shade dissatisfaction* in a newsletter by Harvard University's STRIPED (Strategic Training Initiative for the Prevention of Eating Disorders).
- I noticed that one of Merriam-Webster.com's senses for *orientation* lists *bisexual* first, *pansexual* last, and does not mention *asexual:* "a person's sexual identity or self-identification as bisexual, straight, gay, lesbian, pansexual, etc."
- I noticed that in *The Body Liberation Guide* newsletter (March 20, 2023), Lindley Ashline mentions *fatphobia, fat hatred, anti-fatness, weight stigma,* and *weight bias* as acceptable terms for describing various biases against fat people.
- I noticed the second "or" in the Academy of Motion Picture Arts and Sciences' new representation and inclusion standards for Oscars eligibility in the Best Picture category: "people with cognitive or physical disabilities, or who are deaf or hard of hearing."
- I noticed that *Say the Right Thing: How to Talk About Identity, Diversity, and Justice* (by Kenji Yoshino and David Glasgow) mentions the work of Xuan Zhao and her colleagues on the effectiveness of the phrase "Thank you, because…"

- I noticed a video of Taylor Swift adjusting a bow on her dress and telling her audience, "Just trying to look nice for my guys and gals and nonbinary pals."

I captured these by using notes, screenshots, and emails. (I have a habit of emailing articles to myself with *CL* for "conscious language" in the subject line and a description of what I noticed.) Manual documentation helps new-to-me terminology sink in, similar to copying a word multiple times to memorize a spelling. You can document your observations, too, if the process helps you learn. With some practice, noticing everyday conscious language around you can become second nature.

## Your Inner World

Through internal observation, we can cultivate self-awareness. Because we cannot be someone else, grounding our framework in our specific abilities and interests allows us to sustain and scale our practice.

To begin active self-inquiry, answer the following questions. Examining your tendencies and patterns of behavior can provide clues to what can be nurtured and what can be improved.

**How do you learn best?** If you learn best by doing and experiencing, then explore your conscious style by thinking, speaking, and writing about people and noticing how you resolve questions about word choice, phrasing, presentation, and diversity. Before you research alternatives to words or phrases you would like to replace, come up with your own to exercise your creativity and problem-solving skills. If you learn best by absorbing and thinking, then read literature, listen to podcasts, and lurk in forums.

**What motivates you to change?** If you tend to change due to aversion or avoidance—moving away from something—then choose a conscious style based on avoiding potentially harmful language or choices that make you vulnerable to criticism. If you tend to change due to attraction—moving toward something—then choose a conscious style based on promoting joy, liberty, and healing. If you tend to change when there is a clear path forward—moving with the flow—then choose a conscious style based on amplifying the most reasonable and accepted options.

**When do you tend to show compassion?** If you tend to show compassion when you have undergone a similar experience, then ask yourself: *What would it take for me to show compassion when I have trouble relating?* If you tend to have compassion burnout, ask yourself: *What can I do to sustain compassion in my conscious language practice?*

**What are your typical stages from rejection to acceptance?** In other words, when you adopt terminology that you had initially resisted, what was the pattern? If, for example, you began by rejecting and resenting, and then questioning and considering, and then agreeing and accepting, you can anticipate your rejection-to-acceptance pattern and give yourself the time and space to process linguistic shifts. Your initial opinion does not determine your final opinion, so give unfamiliar terms a chance to impress you.

### *Key Points*

THE OUTER WORLD

- We can practice curiosity by observing the use of language around us without judgment.
- By documenting our observations, we can improve our retention of new terms and uses.

YOUR INNER WORLD

- We can cultivate self-awareness and ground our framework in our specific abilities and interests to sustain and scale our practice.

## Designing Habits

Once we get in the groove of pausing and processing, it gets easier. But how do we get those habits going? In *Tiny Habits: The Small Changes That Change Everything*, behavioral scientist B. J. Fogg writes that a behavior happens when three things converge: motivation, ability, and prompt.[10] This section focuses on prompts—cues—for initiating and integrating behaviors that support your practice.

But why "tiny habits"? Fogg's research showed that new habits stick better when we start small, because they require less motivation. Motivation is notoriously unreliable, coming in what he calls "bursts and busts." But if we can make the habits tiny, it increases the likelihood of success, and succeeding increases our motivation to do more. And by doing the tiny habit directly after an established habit, we can anchor the new behavior to an existing routine.

Difficulty with sustaining a habit is a design flaw, not a personal flaw, says Fogg. To troubleshoot your design, he poses these questions: "What makes this behavior hard to do?" and "How can I make this behavior easier to do?"

To demonstrate how to make conscious language habits tiny and how to tie habits to prompts in your routine, I offer the following examples. Please take a moment after you have read through them to choose a few that excite you, or use these ideas to spark your own prompts. When motivation increases, you can make the habits less tiny.

### *To cultivate curiosity:*

After I go to fold the laundry, I will press play on a podcast.

After I make a cup of coffee, I will read one sentence of a book.

After I receive *The Conscious Language Newsletter*, I will open it.

After I encounter an opposing viewpoint, I will read the first paragraph.

After I launch a streaming service, I will go to the documentaries category.

After I read about book banning, I will put a banned book in my virtual shopping cart.

### *To consider context:*

After I describe someone's traits, I will pay attention to my choice of adjectives.

After I read a novel, I will picture the main character as another gender/sex.

After I notice someone being unkind, I will think, *I don't know what they are going through.*

After I assume that a person of a dominant culture has more privilege, I will note their intersecting identities.

After I choose a word, I will think about its impact on different audiences.

### To increase self-awareness:

After I hear an opinion, I will attribute it to that person and not a group.

After I think or say *stupid, lame,* or *crazy,* I will figure out what I meant.

After I feel surprised by a viewpoint, I will ask myself what I had assumed.

After I read about an unfair practice, I will ask myself, *Have I done this?*

After I notice my fear, I will locate that feeling in my body.

After I notice my resistance, I will take a deep breath and tap. (To learn about tapping, see chapter four's "Self-Care" on page 205.)

After I notice my joy, I will notice the cause.

After I notice my enthusiasm, I will ask myself what I learned.

### To practice conscientiousness:

After I read an unfamiliar name, I will sound it out.

After I learn about a new inclusive term, I will note the source.

After I compose a reply, I will check the spelling of the recipient's name.

After I decide to host an event, I will make a note to research disability access.

After I arrive at a meeting, I will consider saying my gender pronouns after my name.

After I check my videoconferencing settings, I will check that automatic captioning has been turned on.

### To connect with your intentions:

After I see Larry Yang's prayer of aspiration (page xxii) on my wall, I will read it.

After I wake up, I will say out loud, "Today is a good day to practice what I want more of."

After I sit down at my desk, I will think about the most important task today.

After I hear unskillful words by an ally, I will think, *It's OK.*

After I notice a flower, I will stop and smell it.

### To use and update your references:

After I open a style guide, I will locate the introductory statement.

After I learn about a new term, I will type it into my browser.

After I learn about a useful style guide, I will make a note.

After I come across a phrasing that I like, I will add it to my personal style sheet.

***To open gates and amplify marginalized voices in other ways:***

After I hear someone speak out, I will thank them.

After I attend a webinar, I will visit the presenter's website.

After I am asked to nominate someone, I will consider people of marginalized cultures.

After I turn down a work opportunity, I will refer an expert of color.

After I learn about a fundraiser, I will consider donating.

After I enter a library, I will request a banned book.

### *Key Points*

- Motivation by itself is unreliable.
- To design habits that support you on your journey of awareness, you can use everyday actions as prompts.
- To troubleshoot your design, behavioral scientist B. J. Fogg recommends asking: *What makes this behavior hard to do?* and *How can I make this behavior easier to do?*

## Thinking Like an Editor

The practice of conscious language is akin to the process of editing—both are devoted to the thoughtful preparation of content for a specific context. For me, a longtime editor, the two meditations cannot be separated: Conscious language is conscious editing. Because my editorial experience informs my conscious language practice, understanding how editors approach their work may benefit your decision-making process or, at the very least, provide perspective on what is typical and reasonable.

Of course, editors do not necessarily think alike, but editors at all levels—developmental editing, line editing, copyediting, and proofreading—share traits and habits and outlooks that help them be alert to language. By asking you to think like an editor, I am in no way suggesting that you need an editor's understanding of language to use it consciously. This is an invitation for you to peek behind the scenes of an oft-misunderstood profession to learn how you can integrate bravery, creativity, and flexibility into the foundation of your conscious language practice.

**Editors are brave.** Querying—that is, flagging potential problems for review—may draw ire from sensitive or arrogant creators. But failing to query may enable potential problems to make it through to the audience. Every mark reflects a clear intention, or should. Editors must be able to defend their choices, which will most certainly be challenged at some point. Conscious language is very much about having the bravery to use language that respects even if you are one of the few to do so.

**Editors are creative** because editors are problem-solvers. The more skills and resources we have in our toolbox, the more ways we have to identify, evaluate, and fix a problem. Newer editors can often be recognized by their rigid and binary solutions. Experience fuels creativity, and creativity expands choice. It pays to learn the "rules" so you can bend or break them.

**Editors are flexible.** They work within the constraints of time, resources, technology, and skill. When time is short, editors triage their work to tackle the most egregious problems and let the rest go. Editors consult experts when the subject is beyond their experience. Editors weigh a word's optimality with searchability when optimizing content for search engines. Editors accept that a small percentage of errors may appear in the final product. And editors expect some readers to perceive errors where there are none. In short, editing—and practicing conscious language—requires adaptability and pragmatism.

**Editors read widely** to stay current with events, styles, and usage. And editors read deeply so they can specialize and serve niche writers and audiences. It is challenging to edit well when you are out of the loop. Accuracy, clarity, and fairness are of paramount importance to editors, so being in the know allows editors to flag potential bias.

**Editors look stuff up.** An editor's bookshelf is likely to be crammed with dictionaries, thesauruses, grammar books, style guides, and primers on punctuation and syntax, because the best response to "Why did you mark this?" is to cite a source. At the same time, editors recognize the limits of a reference's authority. Modern dictionaries are records of how words are used, not instructions on how words should be used. Thesauruses may suggest words that some deem offensive. Grammar books address the ins and outs of standard English, which is more formal than what may be used outside of school and work. Style guides encourage flexibility and contextual decisions, not unquestioning compliance. Knowing a reference's capabilities is key to avoiding overreliance.

*Key Point*
___

• Editorial principles and practices like bravery, creativity, and flexibility can be integrated into your conscious style.

## Deferring to Credible Sources

A key part of your plan involves knowing which sources to consult and if the advice is relevant for your context. When a term, description, or narrative involves a group you belong to, or when you label or describe yourself, you are the authority on the appropriateness of the language. You do not need your group's permission, even if your choices are in the minority. But when the language usage does not directly affect you, whose opinions matter the most?

Whenever possible, prioritize sources based on their authority and familiarity with the topic, and establish a clear consultation sequence. Give the most weight—or the entire weight—to guidance by the communities directly affected by the usage, then affinity organizations, then service organizations that work with community members. Reference works, publications, and writings that are trusted and routinely updated can also be consulted down the line, especially when it is challenging to determine the practices and preferences of the affected communities.

Beware of "outsider outrage"—when people with no stake drive language change, ostensibly on behalf of a marginalized group but often excluding their voices and opinions. Pushing an agenda from the outside, regardless of intention, can derail a community's effort to bring awareness to their actual needs and concerns.

To demonstrate ways to think critically about your sources, here are examples of analyzing language and deferring to people directly affected by it.

**"Womxn"/"womyn."** Womyn with a *y* was first recorded in the mid-1970s. Because of its association with women's festivals, this alternative spelling of *women* was also associated with trans-exclusionary radical White feminists. In recent years, another word has risen in popularity as a gender-inclusive alternative to *womyn* with a *y*: *womxn* with an *x* instead of an *e* but pronounced the same. According to the Womxn's Center for Success at the University of California, Irvine, "Womxn [with an *x*] acknowledges that gender identity exists in a sphere and one word has room for multiple gender expressions without weighing one more important than another."[11] *Womxn* with an *x* was embraced by the 2017 Womxn's March on Seattle by women who want a more inclusive legacy for their self-label, Black feminist organizations among them.

But there's a hitch: Trans women do not actually feel included by the respelling with an *x*. Respelling *women* for the purpose of including trans women implies that trans women are not women. To be clear, any person can use any self-label, which the Womxn's Center makes sure to assert, but *women* with an old-fashioned *e* more clearly includes trans women.

On a related note: Both *trans woman* and *trans man* are two words because *trans* is an adjective. Merging them into one word suggests that trans women and trans men are not included in *woman* and *man*, respectively.

**"Latinx"/"Latine."** *Latinx* (pronounced la-TEE-nex) emerged in the early aughts as a gender-neutral alternative to *Latino* and *Latina*. In response to the messy origin stories in circulation, Mexican American author and translator David Bowles said, "White people did not make up Latinx. It was queer Latinx people...Our little subgroup of the community created that. It was created by English-speaking US Latinx people for use in English conversation."[12] Though *Latinx* was added to the online version of *The American Heritage Dictionary* around 2017, the narrative in mainstream media is that awareness of *Latinx* is "relatively low,"[13] the term "can't catch on"[14] because it is not needed, folks with Latin American roots who identify as LGBTQ prefer *Hispanic*,[15] and "nobody uses"[16] *Latinx*.

The unpopularity may be true, and that's OK—people who have been marginalized will use language that accommodates their identities and perspectives regardless of mainstream support. But did the reporters and researchers ask the right people? Deferring to more privileged groups about an issue with particular salience to a less privileged group is analogous to asking men if they think women's rights are worthwhile or nah. People who are lesbian, gay, bisexual, trans, and/or queer can be as resistant to inclusive terminology as anyone, so asking binary LGBTQ people in Hispanic communities if they like the gender-neutral *Latinx* fails to isolate the opinions of nonbinary people within Hispanic communities—the group directly impacted. Many critics blame the *x* for being difficult to pronounce in Spanish, so it is not surprising that *Latine* has gained ground in Latin American countries[17] and may surpass the acceptance of *Latinx* in the US. (Other words gender-neutralized in a similar fashion include *Chicane/Chicanx* and *Filipine/Filipinx*.\*) According to Call Me Latine, the gender-neutral Spanish *e* "is native to the Spanish language and can be seen in many gender-neutral words like 'estudiante.'"[18]

*"Fishers"/"fishermen."* In North American fisheries, most women and men who fish identify as *fishermen*.[19] However, initiatives to implement *fishers* as a gender-neutral style are under way. A nonprofit asked for my help in persuading a reluctant majority to replace *fishermen* with *fishers*. To me, the *fisher* movement parallels that of *Latinx/Latine*. So, to make *fishermen* more inclusive, we can add *fishers* while still mentioning *fishermen*. Among the alternatives I proposed were *fishers and fishermen; fishers, including fishermen and fisherwomen; fishermen, fisherwomen, and nonbinary fishers; fishers, fisherwomen, and fishermen; fishers of all genders; people who fish;* or mixing the phrases.

Part of my reasoning for not wanting to eradicate gendered terms like *fishermen* is that if the majority views inclusive language as exclusive of them, it is less likely to be adopted. Instead of blaming the system that creates and sustains inequities, many

---

\*For a discussion on *Filipinx* and the shifting of the *x* to *Filipine*, read "In Defense of the X: Centering Queer, Trans, and Non-Binary Pilipina/x/os, Queer Vernacular, and the Politics of Naming," by Kay Ulanday Barrett, Karen Buenavista Hanna, and Anang Palomar in *Alon: Journal for Filipinx American and Diasporic Studies*, July 2021, at https://escholarship.org/uc/item/7148255f.

people blame marginalized people for shifts away from language they are emotionally invested in. So I believe in finding creative ways to bring everyone along. Sometimes using one broad term is unavoidable, such as in news headlines and other places short on space. But if content creators understand that using conscious language means exposing audiences to a variety of inclusive styles that work with the context, then others may be encouraged to approach language thoughtfully and creatively.

What did the nonprofit choose? Persuaded by my point about marginalized people often bearing the brunt of the blame for language change, they told me they would ease into the transition with the phrase *fishers and fishermen*.

## *Key Points*

- If you are part of the affected group, you can defer to yourself.
- Establish a consultation sequence. Prioritize sources based on authority and familiarity with the topic.
- Be attentive to "outsider outrage," when people outside the group push an agenda without consulting the affected group.

## CHAPTER THREE

# PRACTICE

In this section, I present best practices for when you are in doubt. These are overarching guidelines for consideration, not inflexible commandments. If you have a more appropriate style, then there is no need to override your specific solution with my general one. You know your context best — the source, the audience, the message — and how you can consciously combine content and context. This is why I (usually) ask you to *try* or *consider* the alternatives instead of *use* or *do*. Every time I say *consider*, I am acknowledging nuance and complexity. Likewise, I use *can* and *may* to acknowledge differing abilities, interests, and resources.

To clarify the best practices, I present written and spoken examples, some gleaned from mass media. The media examples can be applied to a personal practice, because individuals have the means to create, distribute, share, and comment on media. In other words, the media examples can help you decide which messages to amplify.

Though the content is intended to be evergreen, some parts will inevitably become outdated. In the last chapter, Persuade, I walk you through building a custom reference stack and style sheet, starting with (mostly free) resources so your sources grow beyond this book.

Before you turn the page, I want to leave you with a thought about words as tools. When I was a child, my mother taught me that old rice can be used as glue, rubber bands double as erasers, and cloth napkins are a few folds from being dolls. I grew up contemplating everyday objects in terms of what they can do instead of what they were designed to do. The same objects-as-tools approach can be practiced with language. Paying attention to what words can do, and less attention to what they were meant to do, can guide positive intentions toward positive impacts and away from using words as unwitting weapons.

## ZOOM LEVELS

Conscious language users sometimes focus on words because many implicit biases surface at the word level. Outdated terms and misspelled names, for instance, can often be identified, evaluated, and repaired at the word level. But limiting our evaluation to words and only words can leave underlying attitudes unquestioned or encourage the misguided practice of judging words out of context.

As a writer and editor, I knew that a word up close could pass all the word-checker, slur-checker, bias-checker tests yet contribute to a biased message. I also knew that scrutinizing a word without taking the larger context into account could encourage knee-jerk binary judgments. So I developed a methodology for detecting potential bias by observing how meaning changes depending on the context. When we zoom out and examine words within increasingly larger contexts, other patterns of bias can and do emerge. What initially appears to be bias at a lower level may turn out to be justified at a higher level, thanks to the fuller context. Zooming in and out helps us piece the clues together.

Context is crucial to anticipating and understanding consequence. Answering questions like "Whose freedoms are being taken away?" is impossible without a point of reference. People of Han Chinese descent are racially oppressed in the United States, but in China, their culture dominates. Christians are the prevailing religious group in the United States, but in other parts of the world, they are religiously oppressed. The very act of clarifying the context forces us to pause and check our biases.

Some of the most insidious bias is intentionally cloaked in neutral words. In *The New Jim Crow: Mass Incarceration in the Age of Colorblindness*, Michelle Alexander writes, "The War on Drugs, cloaked in race-neutral language, offered whites opposed to racial reform a unique opportunity to express their hostility toward blacks and black progress, without being exposed to the charge of racism."[1] Working with content beyond the word level can remind us that our words are juxtaposed with history and that the influence of past events permeates all contexts.

A sensible distrust of word-level meanings encourages us to delay judgment until we have read the whole book or listened to the whole conversation. Proponents of book banning in schools, for example, intentionally decontextualize sentences to bolster their claims that a particular book is inappropriate. But without adequate context, such determinations cannot be made. Critical questioning at each zoom level can restore perspective.

In this section, I present zoom levels as one of your most powerful tools for evaluating potential bias. By introducing the word level first and then zooming out to the sentence, story, and series levels, I demonstrate the power of context and how potential word problems can be amplified or eliminated. Word to series is the ideal order for checking existing content. However, the proper order for planning and creating logically begins at the series level, the stage when key decisions about contributors, storyteller, audience, and logistics are made. When going from word to series, the series level, instead, becomes an opportunity to review patterns and proportions and shore up gaps in diversity.

## Word Level

At the word level, we can check for implicit and explicit biases in words, word strings, phrases, and expressions. Remedying bias may require replacing or omitting words. A potential issue at the word level may be resolved at a higher level.

## Gender-Free Terminology

Gender-free language can promote fair treatment and equitable representations and lighten the weight of gender in our society. By making gendered language a choice instead of a default, we can imbue our words with more meaning and intention.

Needlessly gendered terminology can erase nonbinary people and suggest that potential is gender-based. Instead of *mailman* or *mailwoman*, consider *letter carrier* or *postal worker*. Instead of *spokesman* or *spokeswoman*, consider *spokesperson* or *representative*. Instead of *handyman* or *handywoman*, consider *handyperson*. Instead of *yes-man* or *yes-woman*, consider *yes-person*. Of course, use gendered and sexed terminology when appropriate. *Goddess* captures an air that *god* and *female god* cannot.

Male-gendered terms that are intended as neutral, like *mankind*, *man-made*, and *businessman*, may suggest that men are the norm. Instead of *mankind*, consider *humankind, humanity, humans, human beings*, or *people*. Instead of *man-made*, consider *human-made, made by humans, synthetic, constructed*, or *manufactured*. Instead of *businessman*, consider *business owner* or *entrepreneur*.

Terms for women that are derived from neutral terms may suggest that women are lesser than other genders. Instead of *actress* for women and *actor* for other genders, consider *actor, performer*, or *entertainer*. Instead of *waitress* for *women* and *waiter* for other genders, consider *waiter* or *server*.

Gendered prefixes, such as *boy-* and *girl-*, and gendered suffixes, such as *-man* and *-woman*, often have gender-inclusive alternatives that are more interesting than, for example, replacing

*-man* with *-person*. Instead of *boyfriend* or *girlfriend*, consider *partner, lover,* or *mate*. Instead of *career man* or *career woman*, consider *careerist*. Instead of *crewman* or *crew woman*, consider *crew member*. Instead of *middleman* or *middlewoman*, consider *intermediary* or *go-between*. Instead of *fireman* or *firewoman*, consider *firefighter*. Instead of *lumberjack* or *lumberjill*, consider *logger*. Instead of *landlord* or *landlady*, consider *rental property owner*. Instead of *one-man show* or *one-woman show*, consider *solo show*. Instead of *sportsmanship* or *sportswomanship*, consider *sporting spirit* or *sense of fair play*.

Terms like *woman lawyer* and *male nurse* reveal gender biases about occupations, because a man lawyer is simply called a *lawyer* and a female nurse is simply called a *nurse*. If gender is relevant, *female lawyer / male lawyer* and *female nurse / male nurse* are acceptable, but consider *woman* (or *man*) *who is a lawyer, lawyer who is a man* (or *woman*); *man* (or *woman*) *who is a nurse, nurse who is a woman* (or *man*).

Many gendered terms, especially those without a gendered counterpart, can be made gender inclusive. Instead of *manned the help desk*, consider *staffed the help desk* or *ran the help desk*. Instead of *forty man-hours*, consider *forty hours of work*. Instead of *penmanship*, consider *handwriting*. Instead of *craftsmanship*, consider *artisanship*. Instead of *maiden name*, consider *birth name*. Instead of *old wives' tale*, consider *folktale* or *superstition*.

Often, gendered honorifics, greetings, and direct address can be omitted. In an article for ConsciousStyleGuide.com, Steve Bien-Aimé writes, "Placing a gender modifier before a person's name gives the impression that we should be viewed through gender first and that all other characteristics fall in descending importance."[2] Omitting gender can also prevent us from misgendering. Instead of *Dear Ms. / Miss / Mrs. / Mx. Sara McKeown*, consider *Dear Sara McKeown*. Instead of *Good morning, ladies!*, consider *Good morning!* Instead of *Excuse me, ma'am/sir*, consider *Excuse me.* If female-gendered honorifics are necessary, instead of *Miss* or *Mrs.*, consider *Ms.*, which is free of marital status. *Mx.*, pronounced "mix," is a gender-inclusive option.

**Personal pronouns.** The pronoun *they*, like the pronoun *you*, can refer to one person or more. Both *you* and *they* allow us to refer to someone without specifying gender. If everybody had a binary gender, we would still need gender-free personal pronouns to de-emphasize the exaggerated role of gender/sex in our society. Using male pronouns exclusively when referring to perpetrators, for example, can discourage people from speaking up about female perpetrators.

Having a gender-free singular personal pronoun like *they* comes in handy in multiple situations, including when gender is unknown, when gender is not binary, or when gender is known but irrelevant or unwanted. Pronouns are often but not necessarily tied to gender. Some nonbinary people use *she/her* or *he/him*. People of any gender can use *they*. Some people use a combination, such as *she/they*, *they/he*, or *they/she/he*. To affirm their identity or connection to gender, some people use rolling pronouns—pronouns to be alternated with each reference. Whenever possible, ask people for their pronouns and the appropriate application instead of making assumptions based on their name or appearance. If you cannot ask, defaulting to the singular *they* is acceptable, the way we default to *person*, *human*, and *individual*.

## Names of People

Verify and double-check people's names to avoid errors in spelling and identification. (Also see "Interpersonal Communication" on page 170.)

**Diacritics.** Technology is sometimes to blame when accent marks, tildes, and other diacritics are dropped from people's names. When news copy is transmitted by wire, such marks may emerge as gibberish on some computer systems. But most of us have the capability to properly render and receive diacritical marks. On my iPhone and Mac keyboard, I can quickly access diacritics for a certain letter by holding it down for one second. By rendering names properly, we can convey respect. In "Baseball Campaign Puts the Accent on Spanish Names," Jonathan Blitzer writes, "Stripped of its accent mark, Bartolo Colón's surname is not Spanish for Columbus; it becomes the name of a part of the large intestine. Stripped of its tilde, peña, which means rock, becomes pena, which is Spanish for pity or pain."[3]

**Deadnames.** When trans and nonbinary people transition away from a given or legal name, it becomes their deadname. There are very few situations in which using a deadname is permissible. One is when you have permission. But in lieu of having express consent, it is best to use current names and pronouns, even when referring to someone in the past. According to the

Trans Journalists Association's style guide, which was developed for media use, treat deadnames in video or audio stories like curse words or protected personal information and "bleep those words out."

The names that trans, nonbinary, and other people use may be context-specific. On social media, people use initials, handles, nicknames, or alternate names for whatever reason. Unless you are confident that it is appropriate, respect people's identities, cultures, personas, and privacy by not using names from other contexts.

Deadnaming and misgendering are closely tied. In California, after filmmaker and trans activist Christopher Lee died, officials deadnamed him and listed him as *female* on his death certificate despite his driver's license, passport, and chosen family testifying otherwise. This was the impetus for the Respect After Death Act (AB 1577), signed into law in 2014.[4] Now, officials in California are required to record a person's gender identity on the death certificate and not the sex they were assigned at birth. In 2021, California and Illinois joined Oregon and New York City in enacting similar laws for nonbinary people.[5] Respect for people's names and genders must be shown during life and persist after death.

## Abbreviations, Nicknames, and Shorthand

In contexts where an abbreviation, nickname, or shorthand is common and understood, it is not necessary to explain it or spell it out. However, if it may be misconstrued, using the full version or an alternate description can enable comprehension and empower your audience.

**Abbreviations.** For abbreviations, including acronyms and initialisms, acceptable solutions are to (1) spell it out, (2) spell it out and then provide the short version, or (3) provide the short version and then spell it out. Instead of *LGBTQIA+*, consider *LGBTQIA+ (lesbian, gay, bisexual, trans, queer, intersex, asexual, plus other community members)*. Instead of *API, AAPI, AANHPI*, or *APIDA*, consider *Asian Pacific Islander (API), Asian Americans and Pacific Islanders (AAPI), Asian Americans, Native Hawaiians, and Pacific Islanders (AANHPI)*, and *Asian Pacific Islander Desi American (APIDA)*.

**Nicknames.** For frequently misunderstood but common nicknames, pairing them with the source name can help reinforce the connection. Instead of *antifa*, consider *antifa, short for antifascist*. Instead of *Obamacare*, consider *the Affordable Care Act, nicknamed Obamacare*.

**Shorthand.** Explaining shorthand for complex concepts can help remind people of the original intent. In cultural discourse, broad references to *White people, straight people*, and *men* are often shorthand for *people of a dominant culture in the US*. In other regions, the dominant cultures may be different, because dominance, privilege, and power are contextual. When broad references may imply an inherent status or quality, consider contextualizing to put the focus back on the original intent: *members of a dominant culture, such as White people*.

## Capitalization

In the English language, a capital letter signifies importance. We commonly capitalize names, titles, headlines, trademarks, and the first word of a sentence. We jokingly capitalize generic words when we want to make them A Thing. We argue with great passion about changing a cap style, like lowercasing *Internet*, the global network of independently operated networks, which would make it typographically indistinguishable from *internet*, any ol' interconnected network. (Spoiler alert: Lowercase *internet* won.) *Thanksgiving*, capitalized, is different from lowercase *thanksgiving*, which is giving thanks. Capital *God* refers to a god of a monotheistic religion; lowercase *god*, a polytheistic religion. Website hackers are often anonymous, but only some are capital-*A Anonymous* hacktivists. Trademarks that fall into common parlance become genericized, like *zipper, heroin, videotape,* and *laundromat,* and may lose legal protection. Many people mistakenly capitalize common nouns that have an aura of importance, such as seasons.

All to say, capitalizing — or having the option to capitalize — carries tremendous meaning in our society.

Styles can flex to meet contextual challenges. We use all-lowercase names for bell hooks, k.d. lang, will.i.am, and adrienne maree brown. Brand names like eBay and iPhone retain their initial lowercase at the start of a sentence. But because we appreciate consistency, *baby boomers, me generation,* and *millennials* — usually lowercased — are increasingly capped in mainstream media to match *Generations Jones, X, Y,* and *Z*.

This instinct to apply styles evenly has changed the way

mainstream America capitalizes identities. On ConsciousStyle Guide.com, I capitalize the racial terms *Black* and *White* to maintain typographical parity and integrity. If *Hispanic, Native,* and *Asian* are entitled to the visibility conferred by a capital letter, then what reasons have we for treating Black people and White people differently? Arguments against capitalizing *Black* and *White* bring up the lack of cultural and geographical sameness, but Hispanic people, Indigenous people, and Asian people are not one people, either. And yet, these overly broad and arbitrary labels endure.

Capitalizing also makes necessary distinctions between color and culture—*black hair* versus *Black hair.* Similarly, for respect, we capitalize the adjectives *Native, Indigenous,* and *Aboriginal* when they refer to people: *Native Hawaiians, Alaska Natives, Native children, Indigenous dancers, Aboriginal and/or Torres Strait Islander authors.* And lowercasing those terms communicates the generic sense: *native New Yorker, indigenous plants, aboriginal rocks.* Some deaf people use capital-*D Deaf* when referring to Deaf culture and lowercase-*d deaf* to describe the condition of deafness. Some autistic people use capital-*A Autistic* in a similar fashion—to signify identity and unity. Other identities, such as *Mad, Gay, Bisexual,* and *Queer,* have their own histories of being capitalized, but capitalization has not tipped into mainstream use.

Capitalizing *brown* when referring to people is an idea that gained popularity after a slew of media entities, including *The Associated Press Stylebook* and *The New York Times,* decided to capitalize *Black* in 2020. But unless it is clear from the context who counts as culturally Brown, consider specifying who you mean.

*Mexican Americans? Filipine Americans? Sri Lankan Americans?* Also, lowercase *brown* directly addresses colorism—prejudice and discrimination based on skin color. The facility of talking about the issues that brown people face will be lost if we make it about Brown culture, which, like Black culture, does not align with skin color. One option, which I have not yet seen in the wild, is to use *Brown and brown communities*—if you mean both culture and color. And in my experience, *Black and brown communities* excludes light-skinned non-Black people of color, so avoid using it as an alternative to *people of color.*

## Clarity

My friend has a habit of saying "here" or "there" to indicate a location without gesturing. To them, it's obvious. Not there, *there!* I suspect that this is true of all communication: Only the user can know what is truly meant. The rest of us either think we do or play along. But what if we paused to examine the *heres* and *theres* causing hiccups in communication, or worse—hiccups leading to stereotypes and harmful assumptions? Being more specific can help align our thoughts with one another and minimize misinterpretation.

**Vagueness.** Negative societal attitudes toward aging and older people have caused many to disdain being called *old, elderly,* or *senior.* Those words also rely on biases about who qualifies as old, elderly, or senior. We can clarify vague language by being specific or using plainer language. The AARP favors the broad term *older adults* and takes care to specify how old *older* is. So, instead of vague age-related labels, including for younger folks, consider specifying an age (*a sixty-three-year-old yogi*), a range (*women between forty-five and fifty-eight*), a reference point (*pickleball lessons for adults fifty and over*), an age period (*runners in their twenties*), or an age by decade (*octogenarians*).

When terms like *liberal* and *conservative* carry more emotion than meaning, consider describing political viewpoints or behaviors instead. By discerning between political views and political parties, we can acknowledge intraparty divisions and more than two ideologies. (Pew Research Center has identified nine distinct political typologies across parties.)[6] To heal the polarization of our nation along party lines, we can do more to recognize diversity within groups and not overemphasize differences between groups.

**Euphemisms.** Euphemisms, like *passed away* instead of *died*, allow us to talk about difficult or distasteful topics. But their intentional softness also enables us to hide truths and disguise atrocities. Euphemistic military-speak can make war more palatable. Who among us has not quirked an eyebrow at the term *friendly fire*, which describes aiming for your enemy but accidentally firing upon people on your side. *Defense budget* sounds more reasonable than *offense budget*. And why mention *dead civilians* when you can chalk them up to *collateral damage*.[7]

Euphemisms are also employed when we do not want to commit. Something related to race is racial, but overuse of *racially tinged*, *racially motivated*, and *racially charged* to downplay outright racism trains us to normalize race-based prejudice and discrimination. In "The Racist Politics of the English Language,"

Lawrence B. Glickman writes that this language of indirection "was invented by right ideologues to make it difficult to speak accurately of racial oppression. Color-blind and euphemistic coverage not only masks the danger of racism, it reinforces it."[8] Instead of *racially motivated* and other euphemisms, consider *racist* and *racism* when describing an institutional power imbalance.

When describing sexual violence, consider using stark language that appropriately conveys the severity. Instead of *sexual misconduct, scandal,* or *controversy,* consider being specific and naming the violence or violation. Instead of *fondled,* consider *forcibly touched.* Instead of *she performed oral sex,* which suggests it was consensual, consider *he orally raped her.* Instead of *domestic dispute,* which calls to mind a squabble between equals, consider *intimate partner sexual violence,* which involves a primary aggressor and a pattern of aggression. Avoid automatically replacing *victim* with *survivor,* because some victims do not survive, and some survivors prefer *victim.*

Euphemisms for *disabled,* such as *differently abled* and *handicapable,* hint at the speaker's discomfort with disability. The term *special needs* in particular has pervaded families, school systems, and mass media, adding to the impression that disabled children receive special treatment. *The Mighty,* an online hub for communities dealing with mental health, chronic illness, and disability, says, "People with disabilities have the same needs as everyone else — food, housing, healthcare, education, etc. The difference is not in *what* the person needs, it's in *how* their needs can be met."[9]

## Accuracy

To improve accuracy, pay attention to oxymorons, contradictions, and errors in logic.

**Age.** Linguistic contortions in the news would lead us to believe that children are adults who can legally consent to sexual activity. Assigning the oxymoronic term *underage women* to girls who were assaulted—as MSNBC, CNN, and *The New York Times* did regarding Jeffrey Epstein's arrest[10]—can imply complicity while absolving the men who assaulted them. Phrasings like *child prostitute* and *teenage prostitute* "can suggest that a child is voluntarily trading sex for money," says *The Associated Press Stylebook.* "Minors are not able to consent." According to the National Society for the Prevention of Cruelty to Children, the term *child pornography* emphasizes the materials instead of the harm to children and likens child sexual abuse materials to pornography that is legal.[11] Calling Anna Delvey a "normal 27-year-old girl"[12] (*The Cut*) and 30-year-old Sam Bankman-Fried a "kid billionaire"[13] (*Politico*) may dismiss their agency as grown adults. (Delvey was convicted of fraud, and Bankman-Fried was convicted of fraud and conspiracy.) I myself use the confusing term *young adults,* which publishers, librarians, and authors use to refer to readers in their teens or as young as twelve, according to the American Library Association.[14] What if we used the term *teens* instead of *young adults,* and *teen lit* instead of *young adult books*? Even innocent associations of children with adulthood may contribute to the blurring of boundaries.

**Subsequent generations.** Someone tweeted, "Immigrants: they get the job done."[15] Its author, a writer for *The New York Times*, was cheering Mirai Nagasu's landing of a triple axel at the 2018 Olympics, the first for a US female figure skater. The problem is, Nagasu was not an immigrant. Twenty years earlier, during the 1998 Olympics, an MSNBC headline read "American Beats Out Kwan."[16] The American referenced was Tara Lipinski, but Michelle Kwan, who skated against Lipinski, was also an American. Nagasu and Kwan, both second-generation Americans born in California, were assumed to be from outside the US. What gives? Many Asian Americans are treated like foreigners in their own country. Pew Research Center is not alone in using the nonsensical term *second-generation immigrants*[17] to mean "children of immigrants" instead of *second-generation Americans*. Describing people born and raised in the US as *immigrants* emphasizes an imagined foreignness.

**Historical language.** If you were to replicate a house from the 1960s, would you use products that contained asbestos for the sake of historical accuracy? Many writers are reasonably concerned about being realistic to the era in which their story takes place. In online forums, they rationalize using slurs for so-called authenticity. But unless they are part of the group directly affected by the usage, then they are not entitled to it. It would be, in essence, like replicating a house using asbestos for people whose communities have already been poisoned by asbestos. Why be accurate with slurs, outdated terms, and stereotypical portrayals when every other detail of a historical world is conjecture and fantasy?

Rather than leaning on historical but potentially harmful usage to inject tension or conflict, aspire to create scenes that are emotionally accurate. The impact of exclusionary actions can be shown and told through characterization, atmosphere, the all-important arc, and other storytelling tools. Consider including a note on ahistorical terminology and why slurs are absent to let readers in on your thought process. If, however, your intention in using objectionable language is to avoid whitewashing or romanticizing an era, its inclusion must be meaningful, not casual, with high attention given to the resolution. In that case, consider indicating potentially offensive language in a content notice. (See "Content Notices" on page 127.)

## Overinclusion

Using broader-than-necessary terms is a common strategy when we want to be vague, use fewer words, or cover our bases. But when broader terms include irrelevant populations, attention may be diluted or misplaced. When talking about issues that affect the larger communities of queer, trans/nonbinary, intersex, and asexual people, *LGBTQIA+* is appropriate. But when the issues are specific only to lesbians, gays, and bisexuals,* it may be misleading to advertise the other initials. Instead, consider using *LGB*. When Black lives have not been treated as if they mattered,

---

*Notice my nonpejorative pluralized use of *lesbians*, *gays*, and *bisexuals* (instead of *lesbian people*, *gay people*, and *bisexual people*, which are also valid) here and elsewhere in this book, which is in line with the usage in queer publications intended for a broad readership.

then saying that "all lives matter" undermines the urgency of the Black Lives Matter movement. Thus, overincluding may erode trust in several ways: through false advertisement, by showing a lack of discernment between disparate groups, and by betraying discomfort with using specific terminology such as *Black, bisexual, disabled,* and *Jews.* Overinclusive language is technically inclusive but has the impact of being exclusionary. When we dare to be precise, we can make historically excluded people feel included.

## Misappropriation

Misappropriation, in a linguistic context, is the misuse of words, expressions, and concepts of a marginalized group by members of a dominant culture and other out-group members. It is also known as *appropriation,* but calling it *misappropriation* helps us distinguish misuse from use.* Marginalized groups, for instance, may appropriate dominant culture in order to survive, assimilate, or reclaim controversial language.

Appropriation can be a result of cultural exchange.[18] Many loanwords — words imported from other languages — are considered the product of cultural exchange. English is 80 percent loanwords.[19] Everyday loanwords include *tea* (from Chinese), *glitch* (from Yiddish), *embargo* (from Spanish), *sofa* (from Turkish), *kayak* (from Inuit), *karma* (from Sanskrit), *café* (from French), *umbrella* (from Italian), *kindergarten* (from German), *phobia* (from Greek),

---

*If the difference between *misappropriation* and *appropriation* confuses you, remember: In the context of this book, it is appropriate to appropriate.

and *cookie* (from Dutch). Many of these were themselves derived from or were brought to us via other languages.

Misappropriation, by contrast, often severs, mines, or fetishizes the culture of origin at the group's expense. Other markers of misappropriation include disrespect, distortion, misrepresentation, theft, repackaging, and commodification. Though this topic deserves its own book, there are two main types to be aware of for conscious language purposes: (1) misappropriation of American cultures and (2) misappropriation of cultures from outside the US.

When it is difficult to ascertain whether words were misappropriated, consider using alternatives while you gather more information. If they were misappropriated, giving credit to the marginalized culture in which the words originated may alleviate but not necessarily justify the misappropriation.

**American cultures.** Marginalized American cultures—Native American and Black American cultures in particular—are often maligned and devalued by members of dominant cultures, who then take and use cultural elements and intellectual property without permission.*

According to the National Museum of the American Indian, the concept of *spirit animals* is not Native American. However, "using the concept of a 'spirit animal' while teaching Native American culture trivializes Native relationships to the animal

---

*My style is to use the term *American* when it is clear from the context that I mean the people of the United States. When it may be misunderstood as inclusive of other people in or from the Americas—such as Canadians, Latin Americans, South Americans, or Central Americans—then I use *US American* instead.

world."[20] Instead of language that misappropriates Native beliefs, consider *spiritual ally, inner companion, animal teacher.* Totem poles, made by the First Nations and Indigenous peoples along the Pacific Northwest Coast, are monuments to people and history. Contrary to the misbelief spread by the phrase *low man on the totem pole,* the poles do not place the lowest-ranking feature at the bottom (nor the top-ranking feature at the bottom). According to Dr. Robin R. R. Gray, writing from a Northwest Coast First Nation perspective, these "totem poles were never created to communicate hierarchy in any sense of the term."[21] Instead of *low man on the totem pole,* consider *person with the least influence.* A pow-wow is a celebratory Native gathering. Instead of *My department is having a powwow,* which genericizes it as any social gathering, consider *My department is having a get-together.* In general, reconsider phrases with the word *Indian* that may stereotype or otherize. Instead of *sitting Indian-style,* consider *sitting cross-legged.* Instead of *Indian summer,* consider *second summer.* Instead of *He's an Indian giver,* consider *He took his gift back.*

Much of American mainstream slang was taken from Black English.[22] The intensifier *AF* (for *as fuck*), as in *Black AF,* has been credited to the rap song "Straight Outta Compton" (1988) by N.W.A. The word *woke* dates back to the 1920s, when Jamaican philosopher Marcus Garvey urged the Black diaspora to "wake up."[23] Other slang that has been traced to Black communities, including artists and drag queens, includes *bae, basic, the bomb, cancel, holla, lit, no shade, spill the tea, ratchet,* and *squad.* If you are an out-group member, consider researching slang so that the progenitors can be acknowledged and credited. *BuzzFeed News* reporter Sydnee Thompson writes, "In an ideal world, non-Black people would engage meaningfully with Black communities on a consistent basis, allowing them to recognize language that was invented by Black people before taking credit for or incorrectly using terminology (and other products of Black culture). If, for whatever reason, that isn't possible, then poring over cultural analysis by Black journalists and other writers...is the natural next step before one decides whether to incorporate Black language into their personal lexicon."[24]

**Cultures from outside the US.** When it comes to misappropriation by out-group members of non-American cultures, consider prioritizing the misuse of sacred, spiritual, religious, and other properties, both physical and intellectual, that hold significant cultural meaning.

*Sherpa*, the name of a Nepalese people known for guiding mountain climbers, has been genericized as lowercase *sherpa* to mean "guide." It has also been used for a type of woolly textile, as in *sherpa jacket*. Instead of *political sherpa*, consider *political consultant*. Instead of *sherpa jacket*, consider *fleece jacket* or *high-pile jacket*.[25]

*Guru*, which means "personal spiritual teacher," has been genericized to mean "expert." Instead of *financial guru, gardening guru*, and so on, consider replacing *guru* with *expert*. *Namaste* means "the Divine within me bows to the same Divine within you...This one word encompasses the essential teachings of Hinduism" (Hindu American Foundation).[26] Instead of irreverent uses like *namaste (nama-stay) in bed*, consider reserving *namaste* as a greeting in appropriate contexts. In general, using cultural words as intended is appropriate, but avoid misuse, distortion, and other uses that may be disrespectful.

Lowercase *voodoo*, derived from Vodou, a Haitian religion with the worldview that everything is spirit,[27] has been distorted and used to mean "hex" or "superstition." Instead of *voodoo economics*, consider *unrealistic economics*. Instead of *voodoo doll*, consider *talisman*.

Lowercase *mecca* is derived from the city Mecca (officially known as Makkah), a pilgrimage destination for devout Muslims. It has been genericized to mean "the most popular spot." Instead of *shopping mecca*, consider *shopping hot spot*. Instead of *mecca for skiing*, consider *skiing central*.

## Provocative Language

*Admitting* something or *confessing* something is juicier than *saying* something. By using provocative language, we can add color and drama. But when it intentionally or unintentionally antagonizes, it may get in the way of change.

**"Climate change deniers."** How do we talk about climate change without causing people to grow numb or turn away? Researcher Renita Coleman recommends omitting the terms *climate change* and *global warming* from the news because they are "trigger words for skeptics."[28] NASA and other scientific societies use language that clearly attributes climate change to human activities, with no-nonsense terms like *human-caused climate change*. Instead of using terms like *climate change deniers, climate change* *skeptics,* or *climate change doubters, The Associated Press Stylebook* recommends being specific about people's beliefs: *people who do not agree with mainstream science that says the climate is changing, people who do not believe that human activity is responsible for the bulk of climate change,* or *people who disagree with the severity of climate change projected by scientists.* The lesson here is also to use however many words are necessary to be more neutral or accurate.

**"Anti-vaxxer."** The label *anti-vaxxer* has been used to deride a broad spectrum of people who have not been vaccinated. Their reasons are myriad: unanswered questions, lack of access to vaccines, suspicion of media reports that do not communicate side effects. Among historically marginalized groups, especially Black communities, there is also a deep mistrust of medical professionals due to past and current abuses. If the desired consequence is to successfully persuade this diverse group of people to consider vaccinations, lumping them together and attacking them is an ineffective approach. Science journalist Melinda Wenner Moyer describes anti-vaxxers as "people who are doggedly sharing misinformation and trying to convince other people that vaccines are not safe. But most people are not that."[29] According to *Merriam-Webster,* "The term *anti-vaxxer* is sometimes applied to people who are not against the use of vaccines but who do oppose policies, laws, etc. that require vaccination. People with such views often object to being characterized as *anti-vaxxers.*" *The Associated Press Stylebook* recommends specific language, such as *people who oppose all vaccines or are hesitant about the COVID-19 vaccines.*

Replacing loaded language may be as simple as describing

neutrally and sticking to facts. Instead of *pro-life*, which falsely casts so-called pro-lifers as "for life" and abortion-rights supporters as "anti-life," consider *anti-abortion*. Instead of *committed suicide*, which is associated with *committing crimes*, consider *died by suicide* or *suicided*. Instead of *overweight*, which presumes a normal or proper weight, consider being specific (e.g., *x lb.*) or not referring to weight at all. Instead of *childless* or *godless*, which may imply "lack of," consider *child-free* and *god-free* to mean "free of." Instead of *accused her of being trans*, which may suggest that transness is a fault, consider *misidentified her as trans*.

## Reassigning Blame

When an adjective erroneously implies that a status or condition is an inherent quality of a group, we can sometimes reassign blame by adding an *-ed* or *-ized* suffix. *Marginalized group*, for example, makes it clear that the group is not inherently *marginal*; the marginalization was caused by others. Instead of *gender roles*, consider *gendered roles*. Instead of *token minorities*, consider *tokenized minorities*. Instead of *slaves*, consider *enslaved people*. (Many *-ed* adjectives, like *starry-eyed* and *silver-haired*, do not involve a cause, but due to that implication, the adjective *transgendered* was replaced by *transgender*.)

Another solution is to provide context that reassigns blame. Instead of *vulnerable communities*, which may suggest that vulnerability is an inherent quality, consider being specific about what made them vulnerable (e.g., *people made vulnerable by outdated policies*).

## Exaggerated Differences

Watch out for exaggerated differences, which can be used to dichotomize groups and justify prejudice and oppression.

**Gender/sex.** A classic example of language that exaggerates differences is the term *opposite sex*. Men and women are not opposites — more differences exist within one gender than between genders. *Opposite sex* sets us up to make diametrically opposed comparisons between men and women, boys and girls. Instead of *opposite sex*, which also excludes nonbinary gender/sexes,* consider *different gender/sex* or *another gender/sex*. *Man bun* and *man purse* imply that certain fashions and behaviors are inherently a woman's domain. (This is a double stereotype, because many women do not wear their hair in a bun or own a purse.) Instead of *man bun*, consider *bun* or *topknot*. Instead of *man purse*, consider *purse* or *bag*.

**"Diverse."** People cannot be diverse by themselves, because diversity requires variety. Instead of labeling someone who is marginalized as *diverse*, *BIPOC*, or *LGBTQIA+*, consider referring to a group, which has variety, or specifying identities.† A group may be *neurodiverse*, but people in that group are *neurodivergent*. Instead of *women and diverse members*, consider *women, disabled people, and people of color*.

**"Authentic."** *Authentic* as a food descriptor has more to do with expectation than reality. Authentic to which region? Which

---

*Some countries legally recognize sexes other than male or female, such as Australia.
†I once met someone who had been lesbian/gay, then was bisexual, then trans. So he was at various points L, G, B, T — just not all at once.

time period? Which cook? When immigrants of color re-create meals using ingredients available in the US, when subsequent generations add their own spin, when modern chefs invent foods inspired by their culture of origin, the cuisine is authentic to that point of view, that point in time. *Authentic* is a claim without context and reveals a lack of understanding of how food evolves within cultures. Moreover, it often limits cuisine from people of color to so-called cheap eats while cuisine from White people is allowed to be upscale and innovative.[30]

**"Ethnic."** *Ethnic* is often applied only to cultures and cuisines related to countries populated by people of color. But all people have an ethnicity, if not multiple ethnicities, so all foods are ethnic, including French, Italian, and German foods. The "Global Press Style Guide" says, "Do not use the word ethnic to reference or categorize people in any circumstance. Instead, choose a context-rich description that clearly and accurately defines the shared characteristic relevant to the story, whether religion, cultural practice, language, race or other trait." With cuisine, instead of *ethnic*, consider specifying a region or culture (e.g., *Mexican, Ethiopian, Chinese*).

**"Exotic" and "foreign."** *Exotic* means "foreign," "unusual," "from another place." Calling people *exotic*, especially Asian American women, suggests that they do not belong. Apart from *exotic dancer*, which is appropriate for such performers of all genders, *exotic* is best avoided for people. The use of *foreign* to describe people and languages has decreased in popularity, partly because the point of view is relative: Tagalog may be foreign to most White Americans, but it is not to many Filipine Americans.

Instead of *foreign language*, be specific or consider *non-English language*. Instead of *foreign accent*, consider specifying the region, because we all have accents. Also, instead of automatically italicizing non-English words, which may signal that they are not "normal," consider leaving them in roman type. Or italicize when it aids comprehension, which may mean italicizing the English translations instead.

**Hyphenation.** What do hyphenated racial and ethnic identifiers imply? In ConsciousStyleGuide.com's "Drop the Hyphen in *Asian American*," Henry Fuhrmann writes, "Those hyphens serve to divide even as they are meant to connect. Their use in racial and ethnic identifiers can connote an otherness, a sense that people of color are somehow not full citizens or fully American."[31] Our collective inclination to use *White* or *American* for Americans of European heritage in place of a dual heritage (e.g., *English American*) may contribute to the belief that non-European Americans are less American or not American at all. As quoted in the article, Eric Liu says, "Chinese is one adjective. I am many kinds of American, after all: a politically active American, a short American, an earnest American, an educated American. This is not a quibble about grammar; it's a claim about the very act of claiming this country."[32] Subsequently, The Associated Press, *The New York Times*, and other outlets have dropped the hyphen.

**"Minority" and "majority."** *Minority* and *majority* refer to numbers—or are expected to. Though *minority* is frequently applied to a group "thought to be different from the larger group of which it is part," as *The American Heritage Dictionary* puts it, the group with more than half the numbers may actually be the one with less power. This is true of women in the US—a majority by number but minority-ish by that "thought to be different" definition. This is also true of bisexual people in LGB communities. Surveys by the Williams Institute[33] and Gallup[34] show that among people in the US who identify as lesbian, gay, or bisexual, bisexuals are the single largest group—over 50 percent. But bisexual people experience domestic violence,[35] invisibility and erasure,[36] and poorer mental health[37] (partly due to identity invalidation[38]) at higher rates than lesbians and gay men. Within the LGB population, gay White men have the most power and privilege though they are a minority.

The "fewer than" meaning of *minority* may imply "lesser than," and calling marginalized people a *minority*, especially when they are the majority, suggests inherent subordination to non-marginalized people. These terms are also fluid—a minority may become the majority and vice versa. White people in the US, the current racial majority, are expected to attain minority status by the middle of the twenty-first century.

## Assumed Mental States

Other people's feelings and thoughts cannot be safely assumed. In general, describe neutrally.

**"Coming out."** When someone mentions being queer, it is presumptuous to assume they are *coming out*. Automatically applying *coming out* when queer people refer to their sexuality—but not when straight people do—may encourage the perception that queerness is shameful. Instead of *came out* or another loaded term like *claimed, admitted, confessed, revealed,* or *divulged,* consider neutral terms like *said, mentioned, talked about,* and *discussed.* Avoid *confirmed* and *acknowledged* if those terms suggest begrudging concession. *The Associated Press Stylebook* says, "Don't assume that because news figures address their sexuality publicly, it qualifies as coming out; public figures may consider themselves out even if they haven't previously addressed their orientation publicly."* Similarly, avoid automatically characterizing someone's mention of being transgender or nonbinary as *came out.* When someone announces a new name or pronoun, consider *announced* or *shared.*

**"Presenting."** *Female-presenting* and *male-presenting* refer to appearance (external) and are usually used by observers when gender identity (internal) is unknown. However, *presenting* may imply intention, that they chose to present as female or male, whereas *female-appearing* and *male-appearing* do not. Although both *presenting* and *appearing* (and *present as* and *appear to be*) are predicated on assumptions about femaleness and maleness, we can use them to make observations about sexism and other gendered injustices based on perceptions and appearances.

**"Phobia."** Words like *fatphobia, biphobia, homophobia,* and *transphobia* assume the presence of fear. Instead of drawing comparisons between a mental health condition and intolerance and bigotry,[39] consider using *anti-fatness, anti-bi, anti-gay,* and *anti-trans.*

**"Suffering."** Saying that someone *suffers from* or is *afflicted with* a disability or chronic illness assumes that the presence of a

---

*Full disclosure: I persuaded the editors at *AP Stylebook* to add the term *coming out* in 2019, as well as entries for *bisexual* and *asexual,* which were omitted when *LGBT, lesbian, gay,* and *transgender* were added in 2014.

disability or illness determines the quality of life. As Michael J. Fox once said, "Pity is just another form of abuse."[40] Instead, consider *has a disability, is disabled, has an illness, is ill, lives with*, or be specific (e.g., *has hypothyroidism, lives with spina bifida*).

**"Bound."** Wheelchairs increase access, mobility, and independence. Describing someone as *wheelchair-bound* or *confined to their wheelchair* assumes the opposite and prioritizes a nondisabled perspective. Consider *uses a wheelchair* or *is in a wheelchair* and only when relevant.

## Reclaiming Words

Reclaiming words is reclaiming power. When we flip the script and own the slurs, labels, and descriptors that were used against us, we can strip derogatory words of their power to harm.

The reversal of a slur's impact must be initiated by members of the targeted group, because one cannot embrace stigma unless one is stigmatized.[41] Reclaimed words that are appropriate for use by out-group members include *queer, Black, nerd, geek*, and *mixed* (to describe multiracial people).

Used in-group, reclaimed words like *bitch, fag, dyke, crip, slut, fat*, and the *N*-word can convey pride, camaraderie, or familiarity, analogous to family endearments. But outside of an in-group context, reclaimed words may embody the vibration of meanness, ignorance, and entitlement, so use with caution.

Neutral terms can develop negative connotations through contemptuous or malicious use. Some people avoid the noun *females*, regardless of context, because it may ascribe an inferior, biological, animal-like status to women. Donald Trump's loaded uses of *Mexican* have drawn criticism for foreignizing and stereotyping US-born Americans of Mexican origin. Because some associate lowercase *trump* with Donald Trump, they opt for alternatives such as the verbs *top, best, trounce, eclipse,* and *surpass.*[42] But as Margaret Bruchac, the defender of the word *squaw,* says:

> I respectfully suggest that we reclaim our language rather than let it be taken over . . . We can do what the "Institute for the Advancement of Aboriginal Women" in Edmonton, Alberta, has done with the term "esquao," the northern linguistic equivalent of "squaw" — they have declared that it will no longer be tolerated as an insult, but will instead be recognized as a term of honor and respect.[43]

With the same urgency that accompanies warnings about slur-ified words, we can counter the takeover of words that still have life for us.

## Outdated Words

Words can become outdated when they go out of fashion or pick up too much baggage.

**"White-collar" and "blue-collar."** *White-collar* was shorthand for professional jobs, usually salaried and performed indoors. *Blue-collar* was shorthand for manual labor, usually paid by the hour and performed outdoors. Because white-collar jobs and blue-collar jobs historically excluded women, *pink-collar* became shorthand for low-ranking jobs typically filled by women, such as nurse, secretary, seamstress, and schoolteacher. These terms have become outdated because categorizing jobs along class and gender lines relies on old-fashioned stereotyping. Like many white-collar workers, blue-collar workers can be highly educated and highly paid, with high-tech jobs, but lack of awareness has contributed to a shortage of talent in industrial jobs.[44] Also, these terms may not properly include or address gig economy workers (such as independent contractors), who can be indoors or outdoors, low paid or highly paid. Instead of *blue-collar workers*, consider *industrial workers*. Instead of *white-collar workers*, consider *office workers* or *corporate workers*.

The soft-sounding term *white-collar crime* can trivialize crimes such as embezzlement, tax evasion, and extortion, which partly explains the extraordinary leniency that judges in the US have shown when sentencing people who have committed such crimes. Instead of *white-collar crime*, consider *occupational crime*, *corporate crime* (for crimes committed by or on behalf of a business entity), or naming the specific crime.

**"Slum."** *Slum* is a fantasy, a distortion, a stereotype that blames disadvantaged low-income neighborhoods and not the conditions that create them. *Slum* conjures the image of run-down city areas teeming with filth and disease but is rarely used by people to describe their own neighborhoods.[45] In a *Bloomberg* interview, Alan Mayne, author of *Slums: The History of a Global Injustice*, says, "One of the problems with 'slum' is that it universalizes. There is no one term that can describe the diversity of disadvantaged low-income settlement types. Each such community is the product of particular historical and geographical influences."[46] Instead of *slum*, consider describing the area in terms of poverty statistics, access to healthcare, and other facts. Instead of *First World* or *Third World*, which are associated with superiority and inferiority, consider *developed countries* and *developing countries* (respectively),[47] specifying the countries, or including relevant economic data. Instead of *urban, ghetto,* or *inner city,* which are coded language for low-income and predominantly Black city neighborhoods, consider being specific (e.g., *Black neighborhoods, city neighborhoods disadvantaged by insufficient funding*).

**Medical jargon.** Medical jargon for illness, disability, and other health concerns that is used outside of medical contexts may come across as anachronistic, stigmatizing, and inflammatory, all which may discourage compassion. A person with dementia may be technically *demented,* but the primary social sense of *demented* is "insane." Equating the loss of cognitive function with insanity does not communicate the message intended. Instead of *demented,* consider *a person with dementia.* Instead of *defect,* consider *congenital disorder* or naming the condition. Instead of *limb deformity* or *facial disfigurement,* consider *limb difference* and *facial difference.* Instead of *incompetent cervix,* consider *early cervical opening.*[48] Instead of *obesity,* which pathologizes bodies at certain weights, consider talking about individual health goals. Instead of *high-* or *low-functioning,* which grades and stereotypes disabled people in terms of performance or productivity, consider describing individual needs for support, which vary over time. Instead of *alcohol abuse,* consider *alcohol use.* The term *treatment* may be offensive to people who do not perceive their condition as something to be fixed; consider phrasing in terms of support needs instead.

Medical jargon, like other language, is continually being updated. Instead of *senile*, a vague term that stigmatizes, consider specifying the illness (e.g., *an aunt living with Alzheimer's disease*). Instead of *barren*, consider *infertile*. Instead of *impotent*, consider *people with erectile dysfunction*. Instead of *retarded*, which is a slur, consider *mentally disabled* or *developmentally disabled*. Instead of *deaf-mute*, consider *deaf* or *hard of hearing*. (An aside: According to the National Association of the Deaf, the label *mute*, which means "silent and without voice," is inaccurate. Vocal-cord function is generally not the issue, but a person's ability to hear and modulate their voice is. And because deaf and hard-of-hearing people can communicate by voice and other methods, "they are not truly mute.")[49]

Other jargon appropriate for nonmedical contexts includes *dwarf* (also *little person, someone with dwarfism, someone of short stature*), *deafblind*, and *color-blind*. The words *impaired* and *impairment* are fairly ingrained within some disability communities. For example, several organizations for blind people, such as the American Foundation for the Blind, use the terms *visually impaired* or *visual impairment*.[50] However, the National Association of the Deaf says that *hearing impaired* "focuses on what people can't do. It establishes the standard as 'hearing' and anything different as 'impaired,' or substandard, hindered, or damaged."[51] Also, most people who are *Deaf* (with a capital *D*) do not consider themselves impaired or disabled. So use *impaired* and *impairment* with caution. *Impairment* may have greater longevity than *impaired*: The phrase *people with a vision impairment* describes a condition people have, whereas *people who are visually impaired* describes what they are.

## Sentence Level

At the sentence level, we can check for implicit and explicit biases in sentences, paragraphs, and portrayals that are less apparent at the word level. Remedying bias may require recasting or omitting the sentence. A potential issue at the sentence level may be resolved at a higher level. We can also determine if a potential issue at the word level has been resolved in the context of the sentence or sentences.

## Parity

In parallel contexts, consider describing and explaining evenly or not at all. For example, *Kirkus Reviews* has been identifying characters by race since 2015 as a matter of fairness and duty, for all books, not only ones where race is central to the story. When portrayals are not equally important, consider describing according to hierarchy, such as major versus minor characters.

**Physical features.** Describing the eyes of East Asian characters or the hair of African American characters but not those of White characters may suggest that White people are the standard to which other people are compared. However, uneven descriptions can be consciously used to subvert expectations or normalize a marginalized narrative. In Neil Gaiman's *Anansi*

*Boys*, the story is told from a Black character's point of view. While he is never described as Black, White characters are described as White, which makes Blackness the default.

**Identity.** When Simone Manuel and Michael Phelps won gold in the 2016 Olympics, one headline read "Michael Phelps Shares Historic Night With African-American." By themselves, the words *Michael Phelps* and *African-American* are not biased. But in a headline, the uneven treatment becomes clear: Manuel was reduced to her race while Phelps was identified by name. The headline was revised to read "Olympics: Stanford's Simone Manuel and Michael Phelps Make History,"[52] which is not entirely parallel but at least names both athletes.

Remembering parallels can help us maintain consistency. Instead of *Christians, Muslims, Hindus, and Jewish people*, consider *Christians, Muslims, Hindus, and Jews.**

**Pairings.** Pairings of nonequivalent terms may imply equivalence. Instead of *man and wife*, which pairs a nonmarital term with a marital term, consider *husband and wife* (marital) or *man and woman* (nonmarital). Instead of *guys and girls*, which pairs an age-neutral term with a term for minors, consider *boys and girls* (minors) or *guys and gals* (age-neutral). Instead of *men and ladies*, which pairs a behavior-neutral term with a term referring to behavior, consider *men and women* (behavior-neutral) or *gentlemen and gentlewomen* (behavior). Instead of using surnames for men but first names for women, consider surnames for all or first

---

*Though some people use them pejoratively, the nouns *Jew* and *Jews* are not slurs. *Jew down*, however, is a metaphor based on an antisemitic stereotype about aggressive bargaining.

names for all. If appropriate, consider using terms that include nonbinary people.

**Personal pronouns.** Explaining *they/them* pronouns without explaining *she/her* or *he/him* pronouns may imply that gender-free personal pronouns are not normal. Instead of: *Melissa, who uses they/them pronouns, is an author. They will be signing books on Saturday.* Consider: *Melissa is an author. They will be signing books on Saturday.* It is appropriate, however, to explain so-called neo-pronouns, which are not always new, like *ey/em/eir* and other words not found in a dictionary.

## Overgeneralization

While generalizations with some basis in fact may be acceptable, particularly in casual contexts, overgeneralizations tend to be detached from fact. For example, *Men are physically stronger than women* is a generalization; although some cis women and trans women are clearly stronger than some cis men and trans men, the statement is true enough on average to be acceptable. But *Women are physically weak* is an overgeneralization. Many over-generalizations about people, whether positive or negative, per-sist because they exploit such misbeliefs.

Certain quantifiers—such as *some, several, many, most,* and *a lot of*—can be used to turn an overgeneralization into a factual statement. When no quantity has been indicated, the quantifier *all* may be assumed, depending on audience interpretation. Instead of a misbelief like *Men are always up for sex*, consider quantifying it: *Some men are always up for sex.* Notice, though, how narrowing broad statements and being more precise can reveal inherent conceptual flaws. Saying *some men* or *some women* may make a statement truer, but gendered statements promote a binary view of our world. When gender is irrelevant, consider *some people, a few people, a number of people, a majority of people.* For overgeneralizations such as *Men are trash,* some argue against quantifiers, because *Some men are trash* fails to bring the same attention to the effects of harmful masculinity.[53]

The use of cautious, or tentative, language can also soften claims. They include *can, could, may, might, seem, tend to, appear, have been known to, in general, sometimes, arguably, perhaps.* Too much hedging, however, can make content tedious, so consider reserving it for contexts that benefit from a higher degree of accuracy.*

## Metaphors

Metaphors draw comparisons. *This song is fire!* means "This song is exceptional!" But metaphors related to traits, conditions, and characteristics of marginalized people are often used pejoratively. *A lame idea* means an uncool idea. When a metaphor is used uncritically at the expense of an oppressed group, find other ways to express what you actually mean.

**Mental health.** Casual declarations like *Editors are so OCD* or *That gave me PTSD* have potential to mischaracterize serious mental illnesses as ordinary or even positive. For example, suggesting that OCD is just being tidy and organized may lead others to

---

*So now you know why I'm *can*-ing and *may*-ing all over the place.

suspect people with OCD of exaggerating their illness.[54] Unless you are referring to the diagnosis in a mental health context, say what you mean. Instead of *OCD,* consider *exacting* or *meticulous.* Instead of *ADHD,* consider *distracted.* Instead of *have PTSD,* consider *am distressed.* Instead of *bipolar,* consider *extreme* or *indecisive.* Instead of *depressed,* consider *sad* or *grieving.* Instead of *had a panic attack,* consider *panicked.* Instead of *schizophrenic,* consider *erratic.* Outdated terms that are no longer appropriate in a mental health context are often used as metaphors as well. Phrases like *She's crazy* or *My teacher's psycho* promote negative stereotypes about mental illness. Instead of *crazy, nuts, hysterical, bonkers, psychotic,* consider *wild, unpredictable, confusing, scary.*

**Migration.** Portraying immigration to the US as a threat is a commonplace media narrative and political tactic that causes enduring harm to people arriving from other countries but mainly from Latin America.[55] Inundation metaphors like *waves of refugees, flood of migrants, surge,* and *tsunami* conjure images of American citizens drowning, making it an imperative to control, contain, and combat this encroachment. Inhumane imagery can dehumanize migrants while reinforcing dangerous "us versus them" mindsets.[56] Instead of metaphors, consider *migrants arrive* or *immigrant families arrive.*

**Disability.** A lot of people seem conflicted about the metaphorical use of *blind spot,* because although it is not related to disability, *blind spot* contains the word *blind.* According to my research, *blind spot* is considered disablist mostly by sighted people, not blind people. The "Disability Language Style Guide" does not mention it. Nor does Lydia X. Z. Brown's popular

"Glossary of Ableist Phrases." On a 2019 post in the /blind sub-reddit, which now has 19,700 members, fewer than twenty people chimed in, all disagreeing with the idea that *blind spot* as a metaphor is offensive. But should you use it for anything other than a literal blind spot? A simple guideline is to try out the sentence without the metaphor. What do you really mean by *blind spot*? If the metaphor replaced a thought that was insulting, disapproving, or denigrating, then consider avoiding it.

Other disability metaphors: Instead of *a spaz* or *spastic*, which are pejorative, consider *overexcited* or *awkward*. Instead of *fell on deaf ears*, consider *was disregarded*. Instead of *crippling*, consider *debilitating*. Instead of *tunnel vision*, consider *narrow-mindedness*. Instead of *tone-deaf*, consider *insensitive*.

## Intersecting Identities

Instead of defaulting to a broad term, it may be more accurate and relevant to acknowledge intersecting identities. Here are some examples of how specific language can shift perspectives.

**Generation.** *Teens* includes teens of all races. The headline "Teens on TikTok Are Exposing a Generational Rift Between Parents and Kids Over How They Treat Black Lives Matter Protests"[57] overincludes Black teens, who are probably not disagreeing with their parents about Black lives mattering. Consider replacing *teens* with *White teens* or *non-Black teens*.

**Religion.** *Jews* can include Jews across the globe. Instead of *Jews don't eat pork*, consider *Most Israeli Jews don't eat pork*,[58] but *most US Jews do*.[59]

**Gender.** Women earn 82 cents for every dollar earned by men, according to the US Government Accountability Office's 2022 report on women in the workforce. This average, however, obscures differences among women. When we compare the annual median pay for women in different racial and ethnic groups to the annual median pay for White men, Asian women earned 97 cents for every dollar earned by White men. However, within this group, Taiwanese women earned about $1.21 for every dollar earned by White men, while Vietnamese women earned about 63 cents for every dollar earned by White men. (For comparison, White women earned 79 cents for every dollar earned by White men.) The "82 cents to every dollar" average is useful in many contexts, but thinking about subgroups can be more useful in pinpointing and addressing inequities.

*American women* includes American women of all races. Instead of *American women were granted the right to vote in 1920*, which is false, consider *White American women were granted the right to vote in 1920*. Enfranchisement was still decades away for many Native American, Asian American, Latina, and African American women.[60]

**Race.** When a category is too broad to be meaningful, consider specifying a subgroup or subculture. The term *White people* hides a diverse group of ethnicities and cultures that intersect with marginalized groups. Instead of *White people*, consider addressing the less visible populations who may identify as White, such as *Appalachians, Jews, redheads*, or *people with Arab ancestry*, especially when collecting data for research.

**Demographics.** Information specific to subgroups can be

more useful than information that pertains to larger groups. In "Here's Why Experts Think Suicides Dropped During the Pandemic" for *BuzzFeed News*, Theresa Tamkins writes, "In the U.S., the declines were mostly driven by a drop in suicides among certain groups, including white people, women, and middle-aged and older adults...However, suicide rates stayed the same or increased among Black, Latinx, and Native American men."[61]

## Comments at Someone Else's Expense

Jokes, comments, and comparisons at someone else's expense are generally inappropriate.

**Comparisons to animals.** Animal names, like *bunny* and *bear*, are fine as endearments. But when Alex Housden told her Black co-anchor Jason Hackett that a gorilla in a zoo "kind of looks like you,"[62] she unwittingly invoked a long, ugly history of White people comparing Black people to simians.* To avoid unintended associations, do not compare humans to animals. Even in the absence of inflammatory associations, making animal comparisons is often at someone else's expense.

**Jokes.** At the 2016 Oscars, Sacha Baron Cohen said, "How come there is no Oscra [sic] for them very hard-working little yellow people with tiny dongs? You know—the Minions."[63] His description of Minions invoked colorist and racist stereotypes of East Asian people. Instead of poking fun at a marginalized group

---

*Hackett accepted Housden's tearful on-air apology the next day. (This footnote is an example of centering the person maligned and not the apologizer.)

that you don't belong to, consider joking about yourself or saying nothing.

**Mockery.** The term *small dick energy* is thought to characterize traits from pettiness to lack of confidence to toxic masculinity. Whatever the meaning, it involves penis size. While there may be positive intentions for using *small dick energy*, such as calling out poor behavior, the negative association with size may have the consequence of denigrating people beyond the targeted bad actors, including some trans men and some people with intersex variations. Instead of mocking the appearance, speech, pronunciations, or other irrelevant characteristics of people you dislike, consider criticizing their harmful choices instead.

**Clickbait.** *Angry Asian Man*, a blog covering issues in Asian America, reported that the *San Antonio Express-News* posted the headline "Inspectors Find Dogs in San Antonio Chinese Restaurant" on its Facebook page, insinuating that the restaurant was serving dog meat.[64] The post "inspired a deluge" of racist comments and "racked up thousands of shares." The linked article was a bland roundup of restaurant inspections with a note that "dogs were seen in the establishment." Instead of liking, sharing, or posting jokes that disparage marginalized people, consider speaking up on their behalf.

**Violent metaphors.** Using violence or oppression as a metaphor for something unpleasant may be perceived as deeply insulting. Some terms related to violence (*kill, beat, tortured*) do not convey the violent sense in common use and are considered acceptable, like *I forgot to buy bread. My mom is going to kill me!* But some types of violence and oppressive situations do not lend themselves well to metaphors, even when the comparison is serious. Instead of *raping the planet*, consider *destroying the planet*. Instead of *grammar nazi*, consider *pedant* or *stickler*. Instead of *slave driver*, consider *taskmaster*. Instead of *slaving away*, consider *working away*.

## Passive Voice

In active voice, the actor comes first: *The website provides access information*. In passive voice, the acted upon comes first: *Access information was provided by the website*. Though the directness and clarity of active voice is often preferred to passive voice, passive voice can accomplish several things that active voice cannot. In passive voice, the actor can be omitted: *Access information was provided*. This allows us to talk about an action when the actor is unknown: *Supplies were donated*. Or irrelevant: *The bill was signed into law*. Or understood: *The student loans were forgiven*. But passive constructions can also be used to emphasize what was done and obscure the actor: *Mistakes were made*.

**Police jargon.** Police statements often describe police violence in passive voice to soften the impact and deflect culpability: *officer-involved shooting* instead of *officer shoots bystander*. After police killed Breonna Taylor, many media outlets described the incident in passive voice. One reported, "Woman shot and killed inside a home…in the middle of an officer-involved shooting."[65] When the doer is known, consider using active voice: "Police fatally shot a woman in her home." The headline "George Floyd

Protests Across US Hijacked by White Provocateurs to Start Riots"[66] emphasizes the protests and buries the hijackers' actions. Rewritten in active voice: "White Provocateurs Start Riots by Hijacking George Floyd Protests Across US."

**Abuse.** Passive constructions are commonly used when talking about abuse, where a known perpetrator is omitted or tacked on after the action. Instead of *He was abused by his father,* consider assigning responsibility: *His father abused him.*

## Juxtapositions

Unintended juxtapositions can make common expressions inappropriate.

**Unintended slurs.** *Chink in the armor* means "vulnerable area." But *chink* is also a slur usually referring to people of Chinese descent. The headline "Chink in the Armor: Jeremy Lin's 9 Turnovers Cost Knicks in Streak-Stopping Loss to Hornets"[67] unintentionally juxtaposes *chink* with Jeremy Lin, who is Taiwanese American. Instead of *chink in the armor* in racialized contexts, consider *weak link.*

**Unintended insults.** In a food documentary, someone remarked, "Everything there is subservient to focus on the food." *Subservient* means "serving in a subordinate capacity," and applying it to a restaurant is not offensive. But the chef was a Japanese American woman. In this fuller context, *subservient* echoed stereotypes of submissive Asian women. Instead of *subservient* in racialized contexts, consider *dedicated.*

**Unintended gendering.** Though the singular *they* is

gender-free, readers may infer a gender from the context. For example, readers might assume *they* refers to men in an article about construction workers and *they* refers to women in an article about massage therapists. When one gender is strongly associated with a role or a behavior, the singular *they* may obscure other genders, especially nonbinary people. One way to anticipate implicit biases is to specify each pronoun. For example: *The student is in charge. They, she, or he can decide which restroom to use.* (Shortening it as *The student is in charge and can decide which restroom to use* may also lead to gendered assumptions.) Calling pronouns out every time may become tedious, so consider using this tool mindfully. By contrast, you can experiment with using *them all* like *you all* to contrast with the singular *them*, which can miscue if phrased in a confusing way.

**Unintended insensitivity.** *Come hang* is an invitation to socialize. When Ulta Beauty sent a newsletter with the subject line "Come hang with Kate Spade,"[68] the wording evoked designer Kate Spade's death by hanging four years earlier. When something becomes associated with a negative event, consider establishing guidelines to avoid unfortunate juxtapositions.

## Story Level

At the story level, we can check for explicit and implicit biases in stories, articles, posts, and books that are less apparent at the word and sentence levels. Remedying bias may require revisiting the entire story. A potential issue at the story level may be resolved at the series level. We can also determine if a potential issue at the word or sentence level has been resolved in the context of the whole story.

## Content Notices

Content notices, also known as *content warnings* and *trigger warnings*, are like food labels: They let people choose what they consume. Giving people a heads-up about content has already been normalized in mainstream communities. In online forums, posts can be tagged as *spoilers* so you can decide if you want to read on. The abbreviation *NSFW*, for "not safe for work," alerts you to content of a sexual, violent, or distressful nature. Ratings, like the Motion Picture Association's film rating system (e.g., PG, PG-13, R), help people make informed viewing choices. Content notices are more than a thoughtful gesture; they help build trust with your audience.

When content may be unsuitable for some people, consider signaling it in a notice after or under the heading *Content notice* or *CN* (or *Trigger warning* or *TW*). Common topics that may warrant a content notice include death, violence, self-harm, child abuse, sexual assault, and animal cruelty.[69]

There are no hard-and-fast rules about content notices except to insert them before the potentially distressful or revealing content. Here are examples of content notices and placement.

- (Under the featured photo) "Ed. note: This article contains slurs as examples of how our society and language have evolved."[70]

- (At the top of a section in a newsletter) "We realize some of these [articles] can be triggering for some readers, so feel free to skip!"[71]
- (Under the byline of an article) "Editor's note: This story includes graphic language used in historical context regarding the LGBTQ+ community. Reader discretion is advised."[72]
- (Halfway in an article) "Trigger warning: death threats. If you'd rather avoid this topic, please jump down one paragraph."[73]
- (On a website) "Content warnings beyond this break."[74]
- (On a syllabus) "Given the nature of topics covered, some course materials will include explicit images and language, which some class members may find offensive."[75]
- (In the About section of a platform) "I have Tourette's syndrome. My stream is for a mature audience only, as I say a lot of inappropriate things due to my neurological disorder."[76]
- (In an author's note [such as mine]) "This book contains sensitive language for the purpose of study and clarity, including slurs, stereotypes, and references to death, abuse, suicide, and sexual assault."

## Worldbuilding

Worldbuilding can make the invisible influences and disparities in our world more visible. Commonly discussed in relation to fictional worlds, worldbuilding establishes the rules of the universe so the story has the desired impact. Worldbuilding is needed in nonfiction and journalism as well. Though we live on the same planet, we do not share one worldview. Worldbuilding can help align and orient our worldviews temporarily so that communication can occur. If a fundamental misalignment persists, then the impact of the story is limited to what happened, not why it happened.

**Statistics.** Citing racially disproportionate incarceration statistics to prove that the criminal justice system is biased can unintentionally reinforce racist beliefs if the audience believes that certain groups are inherently criminal. To them, the racial disparities in prisons may prove that the criminal justice system is working. In a report on TV stations in New York City, Color of Change points out the much-needed context missing in the media: "Coverage of crime consistently lacks discussion of factors such as over-targeting of Black people by police, discriminatory incarceration (e.g., Black people receiving harsher sentences for the same crime compared to white people), and the impact of poverty, unemployment and discrimination on crime."[77]

**Proportions.** Worldbuilding can be as simple as providing a comparison. An NPR article on the January 6, 2021, attack on the Capitol uses one statistic to put another in perspective: "About 15% of the defendants have a background in the military or law enforcement. For context, about 7% of the U.S. population are military veterans. Police and sheriff patrol officers make up less than 1% of the population."[78]

**Events.** Providing snapshots or brief facts can put an event in perspective. For news related to gun violence, *BuzzFeed News* included this passage in the body of one article: "The American Public Health Association says gun violence in the US is a public health crisis. It is a leading cause of premature death in the country, responsible for more than 38,000 deaths annually. As of May 14, 2022, at least 15,825 people have died from gun violence this year, according to data from the Gun Violence Archive."[79]

**Achievements.** A big deal is made of firsts. The first African American to play in Major League Baseball, the first Latina to serve on the Supreme Court, the first Asian woman to win an Oscar. But when the absence of precedents was influenced by factors other than merit, consider seating the achievement within the historical context. In *Think,* author and academic Robin DiAngelo writes: "Imagine instead, if the story of Jackie Robinson went something like this: 'Jackie Robinson was the first black man whites allowed to play major-league baseball.' This telling acknowledges the role of white control. It simply wasn't up to Robinson...Reframing race in the Jackie Robinson story reveals white structures of power and the strategies used by those who contested that power."[80] Contextualizing can illuminate a gatekeeper's potential to be a role model, says DiAngelo, the one who changes the rules instead of blocking access.

Similarly, when external influences are a large factor in someone's success, the influences can be part of the story. Contextualizing the role of privilege and access alongside talent, merit, and hard work can present a more balanced picture of success.

**Gaps.** Being responsibly transparent can empower the audience. When a lack of data or crucial details leaves a gap in the story, consider acknowledging the gap to help the audience learn more about how this world works and how it can be improved. The lack of data is part of the story. This is how *BuzzFeed News* made the invisible visible:

> The NCHS report didn't specifically look at suicide rates in people based on their sexual identity, in part because the agency didn't have that information. But experts say this can be a major risk factor, especially for young people.
>
> "One of the biggest problems is that death investigations don't collect data on sexual identity," said Rajeev Ramchand, a senior adviser on epidemiology and suicide prevention at the National Institute of Mental Health.[81]

When we do not know the why behind the what—and we often cannot know, for various reasons—consider acknowledging the limits of the storytelling. Like the ubiquitous "They did not respond to requests for comment," spaceholders are a vital part of worldbuilding. Spaceholders—content that acknowledges the missing or pending pieces of the puzzle—help us build trust and convey credibility. A story about immigrants arriving can note the reporter's inability to interview the families, which directs attention to the holes left when we don't have the immigrant perspective. When the gaps are due to your uncertainty about something, consider being transparent about your challenges and rationale. Holding space for the unknown can help us remember that the picture is incomplete.

Spaceholders can also help guard against unintended takeaways. Studies involving only non-Hispanic White people, Black people, and Hispanic people (the three largest racial groups in the US) can hold space for other racial groups by highlighting their absence, which can help media outlets avoid making misleading, unqualified claims about "all" racial groups.

## Framing

Framing, defined here as "the presentation of events from a specific point of view," is an area ripe for bias. The framing of a story can tell readers what to think and what conclusions to draw. It may involve the assigning of urgency, sympathy, credit, or blame.

Inequitable framing can present gentrification, the systematic displacement of lower-income people, as the revitalization of neglected neighborhoods; assign blame for police violence to peaceful protesters; cover territorial conflict as terrorism instead of resistance; frame the murder of Asian American spa workers as motivated by lust instead of hate; publicize poll results in terms of a small faction in opposition instead of a majority in support; exoticize certain cuisines and customs to otherize marginalized people; and treat reproductive rights as a "woman's issue" instead of a human rights issue. But narratives that reinforce power imbalances can be reframed.

Framing can occur at the word level, like saying someone *had a child out of wedlock* instead of *had a child*. Framing at the sentence level is also possible and powerful. According to cognitive scientist George Lakoff, who uses the term *frames* and defines them as "mental structures that shape the way we see the world," negating a frame strengthens the frame.[82] In other words, countering the frame that *Bisexuality is a phase* by saying *Bisexuality is not a phase* still causes people to associate *bisexuality* with *phase*. Instead, consider using a positive frame, one that moves the conversation forward, such as *Bisexuality is nonbinary.*

But framing as a whole may be better addressed at the story level, because the framing of a story trickles down and affects sentence construction and word choice. The best fix for bias in story-level framing is to research a diversity of perspectives so that we can tell a story that promotes inclusion, respect, and empowerment. Otherwise, we risk recycling harmful tropes, points of view, and misinformation that benefits those with the most influence and access.

## Perspectives

Instead of sharing perspectives from the same few groups, consider including the opinions, quotes, and research of those belonging to less visible groups.

**Multiple viewpoints.** Multiple viewpoints help put an issue into perspective. For example, official reports, such as press releases from law enforcement, may present only part of the picture. Uncritically adopting their language has often resulted in headlines and stories with odd phrasings like "Officers Kill Man With No Active Warrants at Wrong House"[83] instead of "Officers Kill Innocent Man." In *Cultural Competence Handbook*, the National Association of Hispanic Journalists writes, "No news report can be complete if journalists limit themselves to reproducing the authorities' version."[84] To avoid relying on one dominant source for the whole story, consider seeking additional voices, such as the perspectives of those directly impacted.

**Centering.** When harm toward a specific person or group is central to a story, consider centering their perspectives instead of those of outsiders. For a panel on anti-trans legislation, for example, consider centering trans panelists. For a news piece on pollution, consider centering the affected residents. For a broadcast on a hate crime, consider centering the victims and their families. For a public apology, consider centering the people who were aggrieved. For a story on immigration, consider centering the people who arrived.

**Bothsidesing.** Bothsidesing, a journalistic concept, is the flawed practice of giving equal weight to misinformation in an effort to appear fair. For example, climate scientists overwhelmingly agree that warming is caused by humans. But despite the 97 percent consensus,[85] some journalists have given column space and airtime to fringe views, some of them funded by fossil fuel companies, in a misguided effort to provide balance.[86] When the opposing views are fundamentally flawed, presenting "both sides" falsely suggests credibility and equivalence. Another type of bothsidesing is the assignment of equal blame to "both sides" to imply moral equivalence, as Donald Trump did when he said there were "very fine people on both sides"[87] about White supremacists and counter-protesters at a rally in Charlottesville, Virginia. If bothsidesing cannot be avoided, consider emphasizing the consensus view proportionally.[88] Unequal weight can be a tool for presenting unequal perspectives more accurately.

## Relevance

When is a detail relevant? An entrepreneur's sexuality may be irrelevant—unless the story celebrates pansexual visibility. A boxer's religion may be irrelevant—unless the story is about Muslim pride and representation. Details are relevant when they are central to the story.

Omitting relevant details can alter meaning and impact. In March 2023, *The New York Times* reported that in an attempt to cater to Florida's so-called Stop WOKE Act, a publisher of a school textbook eliminated references to race in the telling of the Rosa Parks story. The current passage reads, "The law said African Americans had to give up their seats on the bus if a white person wanted to sit down." But a later version, drafted for the textbook review, makes no mention of race: "She was told to move to a different seat."[89] Erasing relevant details erases the context of racism, segregation, and oppression for Parks's civil disobedience.

With historical quotations, it may be reasonable to presume that male-gendered terms that are not about gender were used as a generic. Due to this understanding, Neil Armstrong's moon-landing quote, "One small step for a man, one giant leap for mankind," has often been paraphrased as "One small step for a human, one giant leap for humankind."

But editing old quotes to meet present-day standards always carries the risk of erasing meaning and, with it, history. "You can't hold a man down without staying down with him" is the famous, edited version of a line from Booker T. Washington's *The*

*Story of the Negro: The Rise of the Race From Slavery* (1909).[90] This quote can be gender-neutralized to read "You can't hold a [person] down without staying down with [them]" yet retain the core meaning. However, the original context was enslavement:

> The uplifting of the Negro in the South means the uplifting of labour there; for the cause of the Negro is the cause of the man who is farthest down everywhere in the world. Educate him, give him character, and make him efficient as a labourer, and every other portion of the community will be lifted higher. Degrade the Negro, hold him in peonage, ignorance, or any other form of slavery and the great mass of the people in the community will be held down with him. It is not possible for one man to hold another man down in the ditch without staying down there with him.[91]

To respect the original context, we can restore the racial aspect to the quote in circulation: "A White person can't hold a Black person down without staying down with them." Instead of continuing to alter quotes, consider going back to the source to learn about and preserve the communicator's intent.

During her 1993 Supreme Court confirmation hearings, Justice Ruth Bader Ginsburg said this about women and abortion: "It's her right to decide either way whether or not to bear a child... This is something central to a woman's life, to her dignity. It's a decision that she must make for herself. And when government controls that decision for her, she's being treated as less than a fully adult human responsible for her own choices." In 2021, on the anniversary of her death, the American Civil Liberties Union tweeted a modified version in a graphic, brackets included: "The decision whether or not to bear a child is central to a [person's] life, to [their] well-being and dignity . . . When the government controls that decision for [people], [they are] being treated as less than a fully adult human responsible for [their] own choices."[92] By changing *woman* to *person* and de-sexing the pronouns, the ACLU unintentionally altered the spirit of Ginsburg's words. Instead of updating historical language that you disagree with, consider adding a side note that encapsulates your observations. It is noteworthy that on the ACLU's website, in an article dated a year before the tweet, the unaltered quote — with *her* and *she* — was followed by this parenthetical observation: "At the time, there was not yet a broader awareness of the importance of abortion for transgender men and nonbinary people."[93]

Irrelevant details may give the appearance of relevance. Describing a victim of assault as *attractive, drunk, flirty, promiscuous,* or *dressed provocatively* may imply that they provoked it. Avoid cherry-picking details to fit a narrative, such as focusing on a victim's arrest record when it has no connection to the crime.

In mainstream news, references to gender in the form of gendered pronouns and identifiers — *he, she, man, woman* — are considered acceptable despite newsroom edicts to avoid irrelevant details. It is a social norm that has not yet been disrupted except in some progressive circles.

## Anticipating

By anticipating questions, confusion, and need for support, we can preemptively provide context that addresses these and other potential blocks.

**Clarifications.** To avoid misunderstandings, consider addressing potential questions head-on. In a *Washington Post* article on the sexual exploitation of female bodybuilders, several photos showing contestants included a clarification in the caption, "The Post attended the event, but did not interview these women on the allegations of sexual exploitation in the sport."[94]

**Disclaimers.** To acknowledge known issues, consider posting a disclaimer. The Hawaiʻi Visitors and Convention Bureau website has this notice in the footer: "We recognize the use of linguistic markings of the (modern) Hawaiian language including the ʻokina [ʻ] or glottal stop and the kahakō [ō] or macron (e.g., in place names of Hawaiʻi such as Lānaʻi). We acknowledge that individual businesses listed on this site may not use the ʻokina or kahakō, but we recognize the importance of using these markings to preserve the indigenous language and culture of Hawaiʻi and use them in all other forms of communications."[95]

**Support.** For discussions of sensitive topics, consider boilerplate callouts that can empower the audience to take action and get support.

- (For teen dating abuse) "If you suspect your child may be in an abusive relationship, contact their physician for help.

Or call the National Teen Dating Abuse Helpline at (866) 331-9474 or text 'loveis' to 22522."[96]

- (For suicide) "Dial 988 in the US to reach the National Suicide Prevention Lifeline. The Trevor Project, which provides help and suicide-prevention resources for LGBTQ youth, is 1-866-488-7386. Find other international suicide helplines at Befrienders Worldwide (befrienders.org)."[97]
- (For disaster distress) "Having trouble coping after a disaster? Call or text the Disaster Distress Helpline at 1-800-985-5990 or visit disasterdistress.samhsa.gov."[98]

## Conflation

Avoid the conflation of words, identities, or groups when it may lead to confusion or erasure.

**Race/ethnicity.** Referring to someone with a dual heritage — for example, *Asian American* — by their race/ethnicity alone (*Asian*) may suggest that they are not an *American*. While some Americans with roots outside of the US identify primarily with their roots, it is generally inappropriate to conflate Americans with non-Americans. In particular, calling Americans of Asian descent *Asians* feeds the "perpetual foreigner" stereotype and may erase a core part of their identity. *The Associated Press Stylebook* says, "Avoid using Asian as shorthand for Asian American when possible."

**Gender/sex.** Socially and linguistically, *gender* and *sex* have become near synonymous. A *gender-reveal party*, for example, actually reveals the sex assigned at birth, not the fetus's internal sense of gender. But in academic, scientific, and technical contexts where a distinction between *gender* and *sex* enables more precise communication, *gender* dually refers to masculinity, femininity, and androgyny (also called *gender expression*), as well as one's internal sense of being a girl or woman, a boy or man, a combination of genders, or gender-free (also called *gender identity*). For some, the internal sense of gender is not a choice. For others, gender is fluid and flexible, in an eternal conversation with an evolving society. *Gender expression* refers to the expression of gender identity, but this erroneously assumes that internal gender is correlated with external expression. Some women, such as lesbians who identify as butch, may have names, body language, speech, attire, hairstyles, roles, or occupations that are culturally associated with men or stereotypically masculine. Observing women's masculinity and concluding that they are men is sexist. A more accurate term than *gender expression* may simply be *expression*, but *expression* may imply agency and choice when our multifarious ways of appearing, moving, and being are often products of things other than gender identity or sex, such as ability or convenience.

To address the ways that gender and sex converge, Sari M. van Anders, the author of Sexual Configurations Theory, proposes the term *gender/sex*. Van Anders writes, "Gender/sex is an umbrella term for both gender (socialization) and sex (biology, evolution) and reflects social locations or identities where gender and sex cannot be easily or at all disentangled."[99] To me, this is an organic solution, many of us arriving separately at *gender/sex* and also *race/ethnicity*\* to acknowledge the mass confusion and the need to move forward in spite of it.

It may be unrealistic and impossible to de-conflate *gender* and *sex*. But in nontechnical contexts where distinctions can avoid miscues and ease comprehension, consider defining your terms. For an article, notes on terminology are typically placed at the beginning or woven into the text. An example of weaving that was used by Michael McDunnah in a ConsciousStyleGuide.com article is "I recognize the shifting complexity of certain terms, like *gender*, that can mean different things to different people. For my purposes, I am using *gender* to refer to gender *identity*, not gender expression."[100]

Please take note: Referring to a transgender man as *biologically female* or a transgender woman as *biologically male*, or a nonbinary person as either, is associated with anti-trans bigotry and erasure of trans and nonbinary people. Also, determining sex is more complex than making assumptions based on the configuration of external genitalia. For *Science* magazine, Miriam Miyagi, Eartha Mae Guthman, and Simón(e) Dow-Kuang Sun write, "It is important to recognize the context-dependent and multidimensional nature of sex... No one trait determines whether a person is male or female, and no person's sex can be meaningfully prescribed by any single variable."[101]

---

\*Many forgettable definitions of *race* and *ethnicity* abound, so I simplify them as: *Race* is the category that holds the ethnicity subcategories. For example, my race is Asian and my ethnicity is Chinese. (Neither are to be confused with my culture or nationality, which is American.) In general, I use *race/ethnicity* the same way I use *gender/sex*: when I mean "and/or," when both apply, or when they cannot be teased apart.

## Series Level

At the series level, we can check for explicit and implicit biases in a series—including bodies of work, articles, episodes, anthologies, compilations, and personal patterns—that are less apparent at the word, sentence, and story levels. Remedying bias may require adding to or modifying the series to change the pattern. We can also determine if a potential issue at the word, sentence, or story level has been resolved in the context of the whole series.

It is at the series level—the highest zoom level—that we can examine bias in the planning of the entire series, stories and all. As mentioned earlier, though the levels are presented from word to series, the actual order is in reverse. Conscious language starts with the concept, not the word. If we start with the word, the smallest unit, too many choices about context and content may have already been made.

## Patterns

One questionable element in a story may not be significant, but a consistent pattern of questionable elements across a series may reveal double standards and other implicit biases.

**Descriptions.** Be aware of the inconsistent use of adjectives: Men are *shirtless*, but women are *topless*. A Black person who wins a game of wits is *savage*, but a non-Black person who wins a game of wits is *genius*. A young person's art is *rule-breaking*, but an older person's art is *masterful*. Children *act up*, but adults *get upset*. Conservatives *boycott*, but progressives *cancel*. A teen *acts moody*, but an adult *is under a lot of pressure.* A straight man is *promiscuous*, but a gay or bi man is *slutty.* Nondisabled people have *needs*, but disabled people have *special needs.* Consider describing consistently across groups.

**Treatment.** Be aware of treating people differently in equivalent situations. Selective criticism, for instance, may be due to overt or covert bias. Media Matters for America reported that in the week after President Joe Biden's campaign launch in 2023, CNN, Fox News, and MSNBC mentioned Biden's age 588 times but mentioned former president Donald Trump's age only 72 times, despite a three-year age difference.[102] Other examples: Opposing book bans except when the book promotes views you disagree with. Editing out hems and haws in interviews with men and nonbinary people but not women. Making a fuss about Chinese restaurants using MSG but staying silent about MSG in Doritos and other snacks.

## Representation

In the TED Talk "The Danger of a Single Story," Chimamanda Ngozi Adichie says, "The problem with stereotypes is not that they are untrue, but that they are incomplete. They make one story become the only story."[103]

The series level is an opportunity to assess gaps in representation, to increase diversity and representation and dilute the impact of single stories. In a series of photographs, do you favor the same races or body types? In a series of profiles, do you tend to elevate certain political views? In your fictional world, do your characters of color and other historically underrepresented characters get actual arcs?

At this level, we have a chance to change direction. After all, a handful of stories cannot capture the human experience, throughout the ages, across the globe. One profile cannot be as diverse as a series of profiles. One episode cannot be as representative as an entire show. Whatever our past patterns, our choices today and tomorrow become part of our legacy.

Here are other considerations for remedies at this level:

- **Diversity.** Behind the scenes, we can hire, consult, and involve people from varied backgrounds—in all matters, not only topics related to culture and diversity. We can read their writings, enjoy their podcasts, follow them on social media. Then, when we create best-of lists, put together conference panels, nominate artists for awards, there's a better chance that we will cast different characters and create new associations. By thinking *diversity*, chances are that we will tell a different story.

- **Intersecting identities.** The way our race, gender, age, and other social attributes intersect affects how we are treated and how we experience the world. Bringing attention to marginalized perspectives can help us spotlight our beautiful complexity. When interviewing Muslims, consider Black Muslims. When covering firefighters, consider female and nonbinary firefighters. When showcasing photographers, consider hapa and other multiracial photographers. Highlight the complexity of the human experience whenever possible.

- **Proportion.** Underrepresented groups tend to be misrepresented. However, presenting accurate portrayals can counter the paucity of representation. Answer every one-dimensional character with a complex character. Meet every clichéd narrative with actual lived experience. Merely showing and sharing videos of marginalized people being themselves can take the air out of stereotypes. Amplify news stories that are missing in mass media, such as the high rates of Black children and Native women who are literally missing. If marginalized people have been disproportionately presented in a negative light—as a caricature, as a stereotype—adding positive stories can provide balance.

## ACCESSIBILITY

Ideally, inclusivity begins with accessibility. We can use conscious words to write conscious narratives, but if people with disability cannot access the content, then how conscious is it, really?

Like steps that prevent many disabled people from entering a building, website design and design for other digital materials can pose a barrier that prevents disabled people from accessing programs, services, and crucial information. In the United States, businesses and government entities open to the public are required by the Americans with Disabilities Act (ADA) to provide accessible websites. Filing tax documents, filing a police report, applying for state benefits programs, applying for an absentee ballot—the ADA offers these examples and more of why communications for people with visual, auditory, cognitive, and other disabilities must be "as effective as their communications with others."[104] These are technical reasons for making websites accessible. But access also enables more people with disability to participate in conversations and be a part of society.

Little acts of inclusion, like using alternative text to describe an image, and bigger acts, like optimizing a website for accessibility, can create a more welcoming space. So whether we create content for our friends, followers, communities, or future self, we can include more people by improving access. In the end, accessible design benefits everyone—disabled or not—because it gives us something that inaccessible design does not: a choice. So let's make access our first thought and not an afterthought. If we wait till the other decisions have been made, applying accessible design principles will be infinitely harder, like rewiring a house after the interior has been painted.

Though you may not be legally required to ensure equal access, making your digital documents and media accessible is no less urgent. Even if you think your audiences have no need for accessibility, they may in the future. Designing digital content to be accessible can help your archives be more future-proof and relevant.

Because many books have been devoted to the topic of website accessibility and inclusive design, I will focus on a few everyday ways to reduce barriers.

## Describing Digital Images

Pictures, illustrations, graphs, animated GIFs, and other types of images share storytelling duties with the copy. So, neglecting to provide alt text for any non-text content can create a poor experience for people who cannot perceive the images visually. Alt text can be read by screen readers and other assistive technology, which convert the text into synthesized speech or braille. (Mac, Linux, and Windows operating systems have screen readers built in.) Because many who use screen readers prefer to scan a web page quickly, alt text should be brief and concise, 125 characters max. Image descriptions on social media can be longer and more detailed. Some social networks, like Mastodon, Instagram, and LinkedIn, provide fields for image descriptions. In lieu of a dedicated field, you can insert descriptions into the post copy or as a comment.

To describe an image, first identify the type. While it may be unnecessary to mention that an image is a photo, illustration, painting, or animated GIF, it can help provide context for the description. For example: *A digital illustration of a . . .* or *In this digital illustration . . .*

Then identify the purpose. To determine the purpose of the image, you can ask yourself: *Why was this image chosen? What is it supposed to illustrate?* The answer will depend on the context. Let's say the image shows a cat on a bed. If the story is about cats, be sure to mention the cat. But if the story is about fabric, then mention the duvet cover. The point is to describe objectively but avoid giving irrelevant objects equal attention. Your description can include people, animals, foreground, background, and the arrangement of objects, including text. If the mood or vibe of the image is relevant, you can describe the use of color,* the shapes, or the angle of the shot (e.g., aerial shot, low angle).

When describing people, I recommend describing physical attributes in plain English. Some relevant attributes may be skin color and tone (e.g., *light-skinned, light brown, medium brown, dark brown*), hair (e.g., *chin-length, in a bun*), clothes (e.g., *tie*), and accessories (e.g., *glasses*). You may want to describe meaningful facial expressions, body language, or the action being performed: *turning back toward the camera, placing books on a shelf, pursing their lips, standing with arms akimbo*. Consider describing people evenly across the board, so if you describe one person's features, describe the features of other people of equal importance.

**Show and tell.** Ideally, a plain description of a person's gender, race, age, or other attribute will allow readers to form their own conclusions about a person's identity, as sighted people do when presented with an image. Unfortunately, objective descriptions may be misleading. To indicate age, we can mention

---

*Some blind people who were sighted can recall colors.

baldness or gray hair. But some younger people are bald or have gray hair. To indicate race, we can mention skin tone. But many people of color have light skin. To indicate gender, we can mention makeup. But some men wear mascara and lipstick too.

If the description fails to capture an obvious aspect, then you may want to explicitly *tell* as well as descriptively *show*. *Kirkus Reviews* uses a variety of wordings to tell rather than show. Phrases such as *read as default White, look White, appear White, are assumed White* indicate the reviewer's perception of race/ethnicity. Contrast these examples with *They are White*, which implies certainty. You can use tentative language to convey more accurately that this multiethnic group *looks like* a family, this person with waist-length hair *is assumed to be* a cisgender man, the two people hugging *read as* siblings. In some cases, telling may be more sensitive than showing: *A person who appears to be East Asian* is appropriate, whereas a description of the size, shape, or angle of their eyes will be deeply offensive. Telling can raise the visibility of a marginalized group: *A person with dark-brown skin who reads as South Asian* is clearer than *a person with dark-brown skin*. *A light-skinned person who looks Latine* is clearer than *a light-skinned person*. But telling might activate our stereotypes, especially those around gender. When in doubt about someone's identities or social categories, consider showing through a plain description instead.

## Making Event Information Easy to Find

For both in-person and virtual events, consider putting information on access and services on your public-facing materials: emails, social media, website, and event flyers. Along with the usual event details, consider including information on sliding scales, public transportation, ride-sharing, wheelchair accessibility, sign language interpretation, gender-neutral bathrooms, childcare services, scent-free spaces, lactation rooms, quiet rooms, food options (e.g., vegan, gluten-free), slides and handouts available before and after the event, captioning, and recordings.*

If accessibility or services are limited or unavailable, you can state it up front so visitors can stop looking for information that does not exist: *This venue is not wheelchair accessible. There is no childcare on site.* Planning and preparing with equity in mind can improve a visitor's overall experience.

## Increasing Color Contrast on Websites

Every year since 2019, WebAIM (Web Accessibility in Mind) has audited the accessibility of the top one million home pages based on criteria in Web Content Accessibility Guidelines (WCAG). In 2023, 83.6 percent were found to have low-contrast text and 58.2 percent had missing alt text for images. These are the two most common accessibility issues. While the rate for missing alt

---

*Thanks to disability justice and transformative justice educator Mia Mingus for some of these tips.

text had dropped 9.8 percent since 2019, the rate for low-contrast text came down only 1.7 percent over the same time period.[105] Increasing the contrast is one of the easiest ways to help your users perceive text. When designing websites, flyers, or graphics with text, you can check the contrast with a number of free online tools. Contrast Checker (ContrastChecker.com), by Acart Communications, allows you to assess the color-contrast ratio by either entering the hex color codes for the foreground and background colors or dragging your image into a box on the web page and then indicating the foreground and background colors.

## Providing Format Options

Providing the same content in multiple formats and on multiple platforms improves access and reach. In the same way that no meal can meet all dietary needs, no chair can meet all comfort criteria, and no room can meet all light, sound, and temperature requirements, there is no format or platform that can be and do everything for everyone. Equity comes from having options. For example:

- A webinar can be offered live with captions or sign language, as a video, as a transcript.
- A podcast can be offered with a transcript.
- A book in print can be offered as an e-book, as an audio-book, as a PDF.
- A PDF can be offered through email, by post, as a download, as a handout.

For accessibility resources related to websites, Word docs, PDFs, e-books, webinars, images, video, audio, links, and hashtags, visit ConsciousStyleGuide.com/ability-disability.

## INCLUSIVE STYLES

We defy categorization. Our variations obliterate labels. Yet we continue to draw lines, build walls, put people and ourselves in boxes. And when someone does not fit, we blame them, not the box. The goal of inclusive terminology is not to break free of labels and ignore our differences. Rather, the goal is to honor the self-categorization of groups who have been denied the power to name themselves.

In light of the trend that equates the broadest terminology with inclusiveness, I want to demonstrate the flexibility, creativity, and practicality of conscious language by showcasing a multitude of inclusive styles to choose from. Whenever possible, first ask people what words to use when describing or referring to them. (See "Interpersonal Communication" on page 170.) If you must describe from observation, do so with care. Labels by outsiders often fall short when it comes to tact and accuracy.

Many of the inclusive styles below embrace exclusive language. By *exclusive*, I mean they are gendered, racialized, or otherwise slanted toward or away from a specific segment of the population. It may seem counterintuitive, but conscious use of exclusive language can actually help us promote equity. *Black Lives Matter* gives attention to Black American communities and their specific issues. Instead of including everybody or targeting everyone, we can make conscious choices to highlight or connect with specific groups who are often marginalized by broad terms. Specificity can open the door to awareness of our differences and, paradoxically, a greater understanding of our sameness.

Note that the examples are intended to demonstrate flexibility in style, not to include every identity or imply equivalence between the terms. Some terminology may be in dispute or undergoing a transition, such as *Middle East* and references to Indigenous people. Please choose language that is skillful, inclusive, and accurate for your context.

## Types of Identifiers

When we describe people by a detail—such as an identity, characteristic, condition, status, or role—this identifier is one (or two) of the following three types: labels, person-first language, or identity-first language.

**Labels,** for our purposes, are identifiers that present one detail or a combination of details as a substitute for nouns meaning *person* or *people* (*Afro-Latinos, pansexuals, mailmen*). They can be combined with other types of identifiers, such as person-first language (explained below). Labels that originate from outside the communities may be useful for identification or categorization, such as in medical or scientific contexts, but may be misaligned with a person's identity.

**Person-first language** literally puts the word *person* or *people*—or equivalent words—first (*politicians who stutter, young adults with Down syndrome, women who engage in sex work*). The goal of person-first language is to emphasize the person and not define them by a characteristic, condition, status, or role. Based on usage among advocacy organizations, person-first language tends to be favored for identifiers related to epilepsy (*your niece with epilepsy*, not *an epileptic* or *your epileptic niece*), alcoholism (*a coworker with alcoholism* or *a coworker with an alcohol addiction*, not *an alcoholic* or *an alcoholic coworker*), bipolar disorder (*an actor with bipolar disorder*, not *a bipolar* or *a bipolar actor*), psychosis (*a grad student who experiences symptoms of psychosis*, not *psychotic, a psychotic,* or *a psychotic grad student*), schizophrenia (*writers with schizophrenia* or *writers diagnosed with schizophrenia*, not *a schizophrenic* or *schizophrenic writers*), and Down syndrome (*parents with Down syndrome, parents who have a developmental disability, parents with a cognitive disability*, not *a Down syndrome parent*).

**Identity-first language** puts the identity first (*American Indian professor, neurodivergent workers, blind women*). The goal of identity-first language is to emphasize the identity first and not separate people from their disability or condition. Based on usage among advocacy organizations, identity-first language tends to be favored for identifiers related to blindness (*blind* or *blind college professor,* not *college professor who is blind*), deafness (*deaf* or *deaf families,* not *families that are deaf*), and autism (*autistic* or *autistic performers,* not *performers with autism*).

Both person-first language and identity-first language are used for identifiers related to diabetes (*a diabetic, diabetic doctor,* or *doctor with diabetes*), stuttering (*a stutterer* or *speaker who stutters*), dyslexia (*a dyslexic* or *auto mechanic with dyslexia*), and quadriplegia/tetraplegia (*a quadriplegic/tetraplegic* or *artists with quadriplegia/tetraplegia*).

In general, people who advocate for person-first language want a bit of separation between the person and the disability or condition, whereas people who advocate for identity-first language find the separation offensive. That means they agree on one thing: Person-first language creates distance between two ideas. Understanding this impact is advantageous, because we can use the structure of person-first language to de-emphasize a description. Compare *Black police officer* with *police officer who is Black* or *police officer who happens to be Black.*

Both person-first and identity-first language are intended as respect, but people who favor one type may strongly object to use of the other. The "Disability Language Style Guide" says, "We are no longer offering advice regarding a default. Instead, we hope you will double down to find out how people would like to be described."[106]

## Broad Language

To include groups that have been historically excluded, we can use broad language. There is a trade-off between economy and precision, so consider broader language when it does not mislead or obscure. *Ladies and gentlemen* can be replaced by *honored guests, friends,* or *colleagues.* Instead of *moms and dads,* consider *parents* or *grown-ups* to include nonbinary parents and adults who act as parents. Unless it is necessary to use the phrase *lesbian, gay, bisexual, transgender, queer, intersex, and asexual* on first reference, consider the tidier *LGBTQ+,* which *The Associated Press Stylebook* says is acceptable without explanation.

When you use identities, it may be inappropriate to turn adjectives into nouns (e.g., *a Black*), particularly if they are pluralized (e.g., *Blacks*) or preceded by *the* (e.g., *the Blacks*). In contexts such as scholarly work in which the terminology for marginalized and non-marginalized groups is treated equally and nobody is diminished, plural-noun identifiers (without *the*) may be less objectionable (e.g., *In the US, health disparities between Blacks and Whites run deep*).

When labels may stigmatize, consider expressing the concept in terms of personhood to emphasize humanity. Instead of *inmate,* consider *incarcerated person* or *person who is incarcerated.* Instead of *ex-con,* consider *person who was incarcerated.* Instead of *juvenile delinquent,* consider *young person in the justice system.*

When using the word *community,* consider pluralizing it (if appropriate) to avoid suggesting that the members are a monolith. Instead of *LGBTQIA+ community,* consider *LGBTQIA+*

*communities.* Instead of *Hispanic community,* consider *Hispanic communities.* However, singular may be acceptable when referring to a specific community: *Pasadena's Muslim community, the blind community on campus, the conscious language community.*

## Specific Language

Broad terminology can hide a multitude of identities. When identities and disparities may be overlooked, consider using specific language to bring attention to separate groups in a way that a broad term cannot. Being specific can also emphasize in-group diversity and disrupt monolithic thinking. *Children* can be separated into *girls, boys, and nonbinary children. White people* can be separated into *people with roots in Europe, the Middle East, and/or North Africa who identify as White.*\* *Pacific Islanders* can be separated into *Melanesians, Micronesians, Polynesians, and Pacific Islanders of mixed heritage.*

If marginalized groups object to being made invisible by broad terms, mention them by name whenever appropriate. Recently, terms like *birthing people* and *people with a uterus* were introduced as alternatives to *mothers* and *women,* respectively, to be inclusive of trans and nonbinary people assigned female at birth. But these terms are not particularly popular among cis women, the group most affected by issues related to birth and pregnancy. Instead of *people who menstruate,* consider *girls, women,*

---

\*Some people with MENA origins do not identify as White. My phrasing intentionally includes only those who do.

and transgender people who menstruate or women, transgender men, and nonbinary people who menstruate. Instead of parents, consider mothers and other birthing parents. Instead of people of color, consider the phrase American Indian or Alaska Native, Asian, Black or African American, Hispanic or Latine, Middle Eastern or North African, and Native Hawaiian or Pacific Islander. Non-White and not White can be used sparingly; they may appropriately describe an intention or point of view, such as a reason for discrimination (e.g., The diner refused to serve non-Whites).

Broad invitations, like Everyone is welcome, may not clearly welcome. Unless we specify, people who have experienced systemic exclusion may assume everyone does not include them. Instead of Great Haircuts for Everyone, consider "A Place for Dames, Gents, and Folks In-Between" (Folklore Salon & Barber, Los Angeles, California).[107] Being specific helps people recognize themselves as part of your intended audience.

**Sequencing.** Conscious sequences can be a tool for emphasizing or de-emphasizing importance in a series of specific terms. To emphasize identities, you can put them first or last in the series. To de-emphasize the perception that order is important, order by alphabet or another neutral system: Instead of Latine, Latinx, Latina, or Latino students, consider Latina, Latine, Latino, or Latinx students or Latina, Latine/x, or Latino students.

**Spotlighting.** When a prominent subgroup might be assumed to represent the whole group, consider shining a spotlight on the less prominent subgroups by naming them. Instead of workers who face age discrimination, consider workers who face age *discrimination, especially people under twenty-five years of age.* Instead of *LGB people experience the same or higher rates of poverty, violence, and sexual assault than straight people,* consider "Because of biphobia and bi erasure, bisexual people suffer significantly higher rates of depression and anxiety, domestic violence, sexual assault and poverty than lesbians, gay men or straight cisgender (non-transgender) people" (Human Rights Campaign).[108] Instead of *US citizens,* consider *US citizens, including residents of Puerto Rico, the US Virgin Islands, Guam, and the Northern Mariana Islands.* Instead of *people of faith,* consider *highly spiritual people, including atheists.* Instead of *LGBTQ,* consider *LGBTQIA+* to bring awareness to asexual people, people with intersex variations, and others with marginalized genders and orientations.

When it is inefficient, impossible, or tedious to list every identity within a group, it is acceptable to spotlight a few and use broad language for the rest. Instead of listing racial identities, consider *people of color, especially Black and Indigenous people.* Instead of listing nonbinary identities, consider *nonbinary, including genderfluid and genderqueer.*

Spotlighting can be used to focus on one group. Instead of *neurodivergent students,* consider *autistic students.* Instead of *children with a chronic illness,* consider *children with asthma.* Instead of *LGBTQIA+ communities,* consider *teens in LGBTQIA+ communities.*

**Centering.** We can draw attention to an underrepresented or misrepresented group by using their identifiers or forming a term using their identifiers as the base. Instead of *able-bodied people,* consider *nondisabled people* (which centers *disabled*) or

THE CONSCIOUS STYLE GUIDE

*people without disabilities* (which centers *disabilities*). Instead of *non-White*, consider *people of color* or naming specific races/ethnicities.

**Additive language.** In the UK, providers of midwifery, perinatal, and other services use gender-additive language, such as *birthing women and people*, to be more inclusive of trans and nonbinary people. In "Gender Inclusive Language in Perinatal Services: Mission Statement and Rationale," the former Brighton and Sussex University Hospitals said, "For us, a gender-additive approach means using gender-neutral language alongside the language of womanhood...If we only use gender-neutral language, we risk marginalising or erasing the experience of some of the women and people who use our services."[109]

In other words, additive style uses *and* instead of *and other* to join overlapping terms. Just as we say *drugs and alcohol* instead of *alcohol and other drugs*, *gays and lesbians* instead of *lesbians and other gays*, *Native Hawaiians and Pacific Islanders* instead of *Native Hawaiians and other Pacific Islanders*, and *BIPOC* (for *Black, Indigenous, and people of color*) instead of *BIOPOC* (for *Black, Indigenous, and other people of color*), additive language joins specific and broad language to avoid the marginalizing effect from *and other*–ing people. Instead of *girls, women, and other people who menstruate*, consider *girls, women, and people who menstruate*. Instead of *lesbian, bisexual, and other queer women*, consider *lesbian, bisexual, and queer women*. However, if using constructions like *pregnant women and people* may suggest to your audience that women are not people, you can either add context to educate or avoid this style altogether.

# Label-Free Language

Forgoing labels may seem counterintuitive to inclusiveness, but words for people are often fraught with stereotypes. Not specifying the who and focusing on the what and the how can help us dodge outdated scripts and create new associations. Neutral descriptions can also increase accuracy and clarity.

**Behavior or situation.** We can teach without being a *teacher*, edit copy without being a *copyeditor*, play the piano without being a *pianist*. To include people who do not identify with specific roles, labels, titles, or occupations, consider using language that describes the behavior involved. Instead of *parents*, consider *parenting*. Instead of *mother*, consider *mothering*. Instead of *partner*, consider *partnering*. Instead of *straight and bisexual women, plus gay and bisexual men*, consider *people attracted to men*. Instead of *vegetarians* or *vegans*, consider *people who eat a plant-based diet* or *people who don't eat meat*. Instead of *a parolee*, consider *on parole*. Instead of *Men at Work*, consider *Work in Progress*.

**Purpose.** Describing the purpose allows people to decide for themselves if a product or service is appropriate. Instead of *feminine napkin*, consider *menstrual pad*. Instead of *maternity care*, consider *pregnancy care*. Instead of *mother's room*, consider *pumping room* or *lactation room*. Instead of *toys for boys* or *toys for girls*, consider *toys for children* or *toys*. Instead of *panties*, which implies "for girls" or "for women," consider *underwear*. However, be aware of reducing people to a bodily function, which may be dehumanizing. Instead of *menstruators*, consider *people who menstruate*. Instead of *lactators*, consider *people who are lactating*. Also see "Specific Language" on page 157.

## Expanding Meanings

Throughout history, meanings have expanded to meet changing norms. *Marriage* has expanded to include same-sex marriage. *Rape* has expanded to include marital rape and acquaintance rape. The singular *they*, which has been around since the late 1300s, has expanded to refer to a known person in a gender-free way. These semantic shifts acknowledge perspectives and realities that were previously excluded at the expense of marginalized groups.

**Ability.** Common words related to abilities—*look, watch, say, speak, voice, read, listen, run, walk, stand*—are generally understood to have meanings broader than their physical meanings. When disability-specific words are used, like *signed* instead of *said*, people with disability may feel excluded not by the replaced word but by the replacement word. Kristen Harmon, writer and professor of English at Gallaudet University, writes:

> Some Deaf writers...are reclaiming the use of "said" or "speaks" in relation to American Sign Language and Deaf literature in print instead of using "she signed" as a dialogue tag. We "speak" American Sign Language, not just "use," they say. "Say" is, in effect, a multimodal verb; one can say, or speak using one's voice box, or one can express, without literal speech, as in the phrase, "the law says" or, in purple prose, "her eyes spoke volumes."[110]

When trusted sources do not directly address specific terminology, we can often find clues in books, websites, PDFs, and social media posts by disabled people and related organizations. From my observations, the words *see*, *look*, and *listen* in these materials refer to mental perceptions, not our physical senses. The Center for Disability Rights says on its website, "Disabled people come from all *walks* of life" (italics mine). Observing content by the affected group can help us come to a conclusion about the acceptability and appropriateness of certain terms, descriptions, and stories.

Likewise, people can *speak* the truth by writing and *listen* to advice without hearing. Deaf people can *listen* with their eyes. Blind people can *read* with their hands. People who use wheelchairs can go for a *walk*. Blind people can *watch* movies and TV.

However, context matters. *Stand up for justice*, a nonphysical concept, can be cheeky or self-sabotaging when used as a slogan for a disability awareness campaign. And telling someone who is hard of hearing to *listen up*\* may be insensitive.

**Norms.** To counter norms that discriminate, people have been questioning words that impose elitist expectations. The ideals expressed by the words *good English*, *healthy*, and *professional* present a privileged point of view on what is correct and acceptable. Some people have been expanding those meanings to include other ways of speaking, being, and behaving. The myth

---

\*Be aware that changing *listen up* to *pay attention*, a broader term, may put the burden on neurodivergent people, like people with ADHD, to adapt to neurotypical expectations.

that nonstandard English is bad English, for example, has been challenged by countless writers, editors, teachers, and others who work with language. Lancaster University professor of linguistics Willem Hollmann says, "Standard English should not be presented in the national curriculum as the only correct form, but as what it is, which is the socially most prestigious form. Saying it is the only correct way to speak puts those children who don't speak that way from birth at a disadvantage."[111] Instead of restricting *professional* to ideals set from a straight, White, nondisabled, neurotypical point of view, consider expanding the word to include diverse hair, speech, clothing, and working styles. Instead of equating *fat* with *unhealthy* and *thin* with *healthy*, consider the fact that health is not determined by body shape or size.

**Social constructs.** Some words with a biological origin have evolved a social meaning. People can be parents without passing on their chromosomes. Someone who identifies as *Vietnamese* may be culturally but not ethnically Vietnamese. Racial identities, like *Native*, may have more to do with cultural and family ties than DNA. In general, restricting meanings to bodies and biology is out of sync with common practices.* When expanded meanings make space for people who have been unfairly left out, it is appropriate to hold this space and not revert to a more

---

*Tangentially related: In *Nix v. Hedden*, 149 US 304 (1893), the Supreme Court declared the tomato a vegetable despite its biological categorization as a fruit. In his opinion, Justice Horace Gray writes, "Botanically speaking, tomatoes are the fruit of a vine, just as are cucumbers, squashes, beans, and peas. But in the common language of the people ... all these are vegetables."

exclusive sense. Instead of restricting *woman* to cis women, consider including trans women. Instead of restricting *guy* and *dude* to boys and men, consider including all genders.

## DESIGN AND IMAGES

In our intensely visual world, design and images can speak louder than words. You may not be a designer or creator of images, but anyone who shares content has an opportunity to check for unintended bias and promote inclusion and respect.

The examples below are a fraction of the possible issues with design and images, but I offer them as ideas for developing a holistic conscious style that extends beyond language. To learn more, visit ConsciousStyleGuide.com/design-images.

## Colors

Color meanings are contextual and rooted in cultural beliefs and practices: The color black in ancient Egyptian culture symbolized death and grief, not evil or negativity.[112] The color white in Chinese culture symbolizes death, not purity and cleanliness.

Use of color, therefore, can be a reflection of our cultural biases. In American culture, common color clichés include using blue for boys and pink for girls, pairing a lighter-skinned woman with a darker-skinned man, using black to conjure negative associations and white for positive associations, and applying palettes to create a mood, such as using a yellow filter to depict a locale as impoverished or polluted.[113]

## Diversity

Diversity is not inherently equitable, so diverse depictions may still be inappropriate. On a Corn Pops cereal box with dozens of anthropomorphized yellow pops, Kellogg's made the only brown pop a janitor.[114] This may have been avoided had they balanced the portrayals and made some of the yellow pops janitors and the brown pop one of many brown pops who are playing and not cleaning.

Certain diverse depictions may be more recognizable than others, such as the portrayal of race through skin tones, hair, features, and body type. Less guessable identities can be conveyed respectfully through the use of appropriate markers. In the ConsciousStyleGuide.com article "Picture Book Images and Unconscious Bias," Christine Ma provides examples of equitable diversity: "[Characters] can wear a variety of hairstyles and clothing, including hijabs, niqabs, and turbans. Or they can have disability markers, such as canes or wheelchairs, service animals, prosthetic limbs, or hearing aids."[115]

Diversity can also be depicted through tasks, relationships, and occupations. Pairing people with behaviors that are against stereotype can help emphasize individual potential. Exploring diversity within a subgroup—such as facial diversity within an ethnicity, body diversity within a gender, and height diversity between couples—can help present a fuller spectrum of humankind.

Visit ConsciousStyleGuide.com/design-images for a directory of free-or-fee stock photo databases that feature diverse representations.

## Associations

Be aware of unintended associations that reinforce bias against specific groups. A hospital tweet using an image of a boy of East Asian descent to talk about the coronavirus may perpetuate the racist association between Chinese people and Covid-19. Fictional monsters that resemble people with a limb or facial difference may connote that people who are different are scary.[116] Illustrations of monkeys in picture books have long been called out for their racist undertones. For example, the Curious George series, about a little monkey who is abducted by a man in a yellow hat, has parallels to the enslavement of African people.[117]

## Historical Content

Instead of banning historical films or excising potentially distressful footage, consider contextualizing them. In 2011, community members threatened to boycott a screening by the Brooklyn Bridge Park Conservancy of *Breakfast at Tiffany's*, which shows

Mickey Rooney wearing yellowface to play Mr. Yunioshi. In response to concerns that the racist portrayal was being shown without any context, the conservancy said that prior to the screening, they would present a documentary by Media Action Network for Asian Americans that addressed it.[118]

## Photos and Videos

Photos, videos, and other images that show people require special care.

**Mix-ups.** *Rolling Stone* mixed up Kimiko Glenn and Lori Tan Chinn, the only two Asian American characters on *Orange Is the New Black*. *People* magazine used a stock photo of a woman of Asian descent and said it was Google Glass marketing manager Amanda Rosenberg. Mistakes like this happen with people of all races. Verifying their identity on their website and double-checking that the correct photo is paired with the correct name can help you avoid mistakes.

**Digital blackface.** *Digital blackface* refers to images of Black people, usually in the form of a reaction GIF, used by non-Black people to express an exaggerated emotion or personality. If you are not Black, consider using GIFs featuring people of your own race or members of a racially overrepresented group to avoid the digital version of a minstrel show.

**Mug shots.** In news coverage, often mug shots are used for suspects who are Black or brown, while yearbook photos are used for suspects who are White. Media outlets sometimes publish social media photos that show victims of color in a negative light even though they are the victims. To avoid perpetuating bias, consider using equivalent photos.

**Inspiration porn.** *Inspiration porn** refers to images that objectify and exploit disabled people for the pleasure and self-congratulation of nondisabled people. Whether they show disabled people doing ordinary tasks or a nondisabled person performing a good deed for a disabled person, inspiration porn may initially appear positive and inspirational to some but actually increases negative attitudes toward disability.[119] Promoting a disabled person's perspective is more respectful and appropriate than promoting a nondisabled person's view of disabled people.

**Trauma porn.** The constant reel of anti-Black violence in news feeds can cause or exacerbate psychological distress and PTSD.[120] Even if the intent is to raise awareness of police brutality against marginalized people, sharing these violent images can increase Black people's exposure to them.

Similarly, attempts to reduce disablism by sharing images of exclusionary behavior, such as students appearing to ignore a girl in a wheelchair while they engage in a group activity, may retraumatize disabled people who have had similar experiences. In *Forbes*, Andrew Pulrang writes, "Even the most involved and committed allies should always be aware of the potential of taking over and derailing disability discourse in ways that can do more harm than good."[121] Also, sharing without the subject's permission is inappropriate and possibly exploitative.

---

*The term *inspiration porn* was popularized by comedian and disability advocate Stella Young. Her TED Talk "I'm Not Your Inspiration, Thank You Very Much" can be found on TED.com.

# Typefaces

English typography inspired by Chinese brushstrokes, known as *chop suey fonts*, has been used by people of Chinese and non-Chinese descent alike to add flair to advertisements, products, and restaurant signage. The problem is that, historically, this stylized type has been used to stoke xenophobia. Two examples: Texaco created a series of World War II posters that featured chop suey fonts alongside a bucktoothed, slit-eyed caricature of a Japanese man.[122] In 2002, Abercrombie & Fitch had a T-shirt line featuring chop suey fonts along with wordplay such as "Wong Brothers Laundry Service: Two Wongs Can Make It White."[123] Consider avoiding culturally coded typefaces when the impact is stereotyping and otherizing.

## INTERPERSONAL COMMUNICATION

Interpersonal communication is an essential skill that can take a lifetime of practice. Getting along often comes down to how well we navigate power dynamics, emotional needs, and unknown sensitivities, so respectful language requires a higher level of tact. Inability to communicate may affect your ability to be in community with other people, which may alter the course of your friendships, your profession, and your life. This round of tips focuses on promoting well-being by using language to respect.

## How to Ask About Social Attributes

Before asking someone to identify their age, gender/sex, race/ethnicity, spirituality, relationship, or other social attribute, pause and ask yourself: *Is it relevant? Is it invasive? How might it make them feel?* You might think that one question can't hurt, but exclusionary behaviors harm through accumulation. Because many marginalized people are leery of being othered, asking may be alienating in itself. Some people are vocal about being sick and tired of educating people about their identities, cultures, and subcultures. But others welcome questions. Supreme Court justice Sonia Sotomayor wrote a picture book called *Just Ask! Be Different, Be Brave, Be You* (illustrated by Rafael López) that encourages children to act on their curiosity about others by asking. But as she notes in the beginning of her book, "Not everyone is comfortable answering questions about themselves." Some critics of her approach may prefer a book titled *Don't Ask Me.*

But asking is preferable to assuming (and getting it wrong). Some people who transition their gender identity maintain the same outward appearance. Some people who appear multiracial or multiethnic identify with only one culture. Some people identify with a sexual orientation that does not reflect their sexual behavior. We cannot draw definitive conclusions about ethnicity based on surname, gender based on first name, orientation based on one's company, marital status based on ring-wearing, country of origin based on accent, or any of these based on appearance.

This is not due to ignorance on your part or deception on their part but to the inherent complexity and fluidity of identity. We can guess, but that has obvious risks. People who brag about having excellent gaydar or queerdar — the ability to sense that someone is gay or queer based on observation — are just guessing based on overt and subtle stereotypes. For identity, people often use different words for the same group, such as *Native, Native American, American Indian,* and *Indigenous American.* Unless we ask, we won't know which term they prefer or if they prefer specifying their Native nation. The best course of action is to get comfortable with asking.

Questions by nature are potentially aggravating, because asking is throwing someone a ball and expecting them to throw it back. Members of marginalized groups may perceive questions about their ethnicity or sexuality as otherizing, and answering them as emotional labor. If you need to ask, there are ways of mitigating the impact of unwanted questions. You can, for example, first request permission to ask. By checking in, this bit of preparatory context can help decrease the bluntness. In my experience, if I ask, *Do you mind if I ask about your ethnic background?,* people will usually answer the not-yet-asked question. But if you need to ask explicitly, avoid saying, *What are you?* This phrasing suggests that they are a *what* instead of a *who*. Though it is shorthand for *What ethnicity are you?*, even the full version may unintentionally equate a person with a detail. Instead, try *What is your ethnicity?*

Consider using the power of length and pacing when asking sensitive questions. By using more words, we can help the receiver mentally prepare themselves. Notice the decreasing bluntness of these questions as the length increases: *Are you queer? What is your sexual orientation? How would you describe your sexuality? Would you mind if I asked about your sexual orientation?*\*

In general, I would advise not singling people out based on a perceived social attribute, but there are exceptions. At a nearly all-White conference years ago, I heard rumors that another Asian American woman was there. So during the banquet, I went from table to table until I found her. I went up and said, "I heard there was another Asian American woman here, so I hope you don't mind that I came over to say hi." And her response was "Did you know there's an Asian American guy here too?" To this day, the three of us are friends. So that is one exception to my guidance: equity. If you are seeking community or solidarity with another marginalized person, singling them out may be worth the potential offense.

**Respecting identity.** Avoid correcting someone's identity. While visiting my alma mater a few years back, I learned that a prospective student had identified himself as Latino to some residents. They told him that he was not *Latino* but *Latinx*. My heart

---

\*The power of length can be used to deliver bad news. The editor of one of my picture books used 424 words to tell me that the release had been delayed for a year, which helped me process the news.

sank. Self-naming is our right. It is empowering. So when we override the words, names, pronouns, spellings, and pronunciations that people use for themselves, we may be taking from them part of their identity.

Along with valuing self-labels, we can also respect self-descriptions and reclamations. Be aware of when your insistence upon a word may be imposing an unreasonable standard upon someone else, like *Latinx* when someone prefers *Latino*. Respect for labels means all self-labels, not just the ones you agree with.

There is at least one major exception. It is inappropriate for people outside of a group to identify as a member. More to the point, a White person who identifies as a Black person—ethnically or culturally—will be questioned. Anyone can, though, explore options that are available to them, such as a non-binary person exploring a male identity or a gay person exploring a bisexual identity.

## How to Ask for Names and Pronouns

To ask for someone's name, consider introducing yourself first. If you did not catch their name, that's OK. There is no shame in re-asking: *Would you mind saying it again? How do you spell that? I want to make sure I get it right.* I personally struggle with understanding names aurally, but I am unabashed in asking for clarification. By re-asking, we may be causing offense, but the other option is to risk getting names wrong, which is worse.

In general, avoid using nicknames or previous names without permission. Previous names may be deadnames and therefore harmful to use, and unwanted nicknames are disrespectful. In any case, use approved names only.

Pronounce people's names the way they pronounce them. Do not ask people to "Americanize" or shorten their names. Do not say, *Oh, that's too hard for me. How about I just call you* _____. Do not tell them they are pronouncing it wrong if it differs from your experience. Be aware of hyperforeignization, making a word sound more foreign than it is. For example, please do not pronounce my surname, Yin, with a Mandarin tone; say it in English as I do.

To ask for someone's personal pronouns, consider saying yours first if you are comfortable doing so. I personally dislike disclosing my pronouns when people know nothing else about me. So please avoid pressuring people into sharing. (This applies to many things.) Although many people use more than one set of gender pronouns, like *she/her plus they/them* or *they/them plus ey/em*, calling them "preferred pronouns" is inappropriate. It implies that gender is a choice when, for some, it is an innate and fixed sense.

Try to ask for pronouns evenly and not only when people appear trans or androgynous to you. Pronouns are not necessarily aligned with gender identity or expression. Many people who are not trans use *they/them* pronouns. If someone's pronouns are unknown, you can either default to *they/them* or simply repeat their name.

## How to Ask Offensive Questions

Sometimes we need to ask offensive questions. What might make a question offensive? Assumptions. How do we make a question less offensive? By acknowledging the assumptions.

As a queer woman of Chinese descent in America, I have been on the receiving end of many otherizing questions, and I am here to tell you about the most successful offensive question ever asked of me. At an ad agency where I was an editor, a coworker came to my office and asked: "Karen, I'm really sorry, but do you mind if I ask you a question about Chinese? We're trying to figure out what the art says before we ship, but we couldn't find anyone else. I don't mean to stereotype you, and I understand if you don't want to be involved."

It turns out that I couldn't help, because I can't read Chinese. But I have been thinking about her approach ever since. It was so refreshing. I took her question apart to figure out why I felt respected.

1.  She said my name: *Karen*
2.  She apologized: *I'm really sorry*
3.  She asked for (and immediately received) my consent: *do you mind if I ask you a question*
4.  She told me what it was regarding, so I didn't have to commit without context: *about Chinese? We're trying to figure out what the art says*
5.  She explained the urgency and desperation: *before we ship*

6. She told me that they took other steps: *we couldn't find anyone else*
7. She demonstrated awareness of historical context: *I don't mean to stereotype you*
8. And she made it clear I had a choice and she wasn't trying to leverage her higher status: *I understand if you don't want to be involved*

In short, it was charming because she demonstrated her awareness that the question was potentially offensive.

But years later, I realized that I had completely missed the real reason why her plea worked, because I was viewing it as an isolated incident. Examining this transaction within the greater context explains what helped this request land right. The greater context is that we had a good rapport.

She valued my opinions on a wide range of general issues, not just diversity. She treated me like a person and not a representative of my ethnicity. She took my concerns seriously. She appreciated my contributions. And she treated me like an equal and valued member of the team.

So I cannot stress enough the importance of building rapport. A big part of conscious language is learning to develop the context that would support sensitive content, which includes investing in relationships so tricky conversations can unfurl. Conscious language means conscious inclusion and respect from the start and not when you need something.

## How to Word a Request

For some people, loaded questions can be deeply aggravating. Here are tips for rethinking phrasing that may unwittingly create a rift or doubt in your relationship.

Questions that begin with *can't you*, *don't you*, or *shouldn't you* may be perceived as masking hostility. For some people, this is a normal way of talking and no hostility is intended. But that may not change the impact. Changing the form from negative to positive can often make it clear why it felt loaded in the first place. Instead of *Can't you find out?*, try *Can you find out?* It transforms a judgment into a question about ability and capacity. Questions are often statements in disguise. *Can't you find out?* as a statement might be *I wish you would take more initiative.* By contrast, *Can you find out?* might be *I am in over my head, and I need your help.* If we can tease out the hidden statement for our own enlightenment, then we can expand our understanding of what makes us tick. Oftentimes, we are not aware of our emotions or biases till they surface through language.

If a word itself is objectionable, changing the negative phrasing may not be enough. A lot of people, for example, have strong feelings about the word *should*. Changing *Shouldn't you be at work?* to *Should you be at work?* may not make it more acceptable.

Even if we phrase statements and questions as nonjudgmentally as possible, they may develop a negative association over time. Our best and most neutral attempts may be perceived as passive-aggressive if that is the recipient's learned association. *Per your last email*, for example, may be perceived as a personal attack by people who associate it with criticism. So if you can, and if it is appropriate, try being assertive and sincere, whatever that means for you, instead of using stock phrases that may have become skunked.

*Can you just* is another hostile-sounding wording: *Can you just wait?* The word *just* used in this context can be perceived as dismissive, because many people cannot "just" do something, especially if they do not have the time, tools, or energy. Instead of *Can you just wait?*, try *Are you able to wait?* The phrasing *Are you able to* makes it clear that you are inquiring about ability or bandwidth, whereas *Can you just* may sound like an insensitive demand.

## How to Speak Up

Maybe you've been there: A White teenager jokes about having "chinky eyes" in a selfie. Your cisgender boss makes a transphobic remark, and everybody laughs. You hear a stranger mock someone's appearance.

What can we do? Should we say something?

When casual ignorance and intolerance surface as we go about our daily lives, it is important to remember one thing: If we do something about it, we can make an impact.

The Southern Poverty Law Center's online "Speak Up: Responding to Everyday Bigotry" offers guidance on what to say and do to fight hate and mistreatment.[124] (SPLC is the organization behind the Learning for Justice project, formerly called Teaching Tolerance.) Examples of conscious speech and conscious action are presented as possible responses to specific types of bias, which can be adapted for any situation where we must speak up for ourselves or in defense of others.

The first step in the "Six Steps to Speaking Up Against Everyday Bigotry" section is "Be ready," and this advice is crucial: "You know another moment like this will happen, so prepare yourself for it. Think of yourself as the one who will speak up. Promise yourself not to remain silent."

Fortunately, there are many ways for us to model kindness, open-mindedness, and boundaries through language. Here are a few examples from "Speak Up."

### At work:

- (To a coworker) "You know, you're giving Democrats a bad name when you make sweeping generalizations about Republicans."
- (To your boss) "A lot of different kinds of people work for you, and for this company. We come to work every day and give you our best. What you just said, does it really honor me and the other people here?"

### At a social event:

- (About a mean joke) "I'm sorry; what's so funny?"

### At a store:

- (About rude service) "I deserve to be treated with respect in an establishment where I spend money."

### With family:

- (About impact) "Your 'jokes' are putting unnecessary distance between us; I worry they'll end up doing irreparable harm. I want to make sure those 'jokes' don't damage our relationship."

### With ourselves:

We can work on our own biases by:

- Exercising self-criticism.
- Apologizing immediately for voicing harmful assumptions about a group of people.
- Understanding the prejudices present in our choice of words.

This is a lot to think about, because fighting bias, including our own, requires intention and commitment. As Bob Carolla, spokesperson for the National Alliance on Mental Illness, says, "If you don't speak up, you're surrendering part of yourself. You're letting bigotry win."[125]

Note: Always assess your comfort level and physical safety before you choose to take a risk. "Speak Up" has multiple examples of expressing disapproval with your eyes and body language when that may be more effective than being confrontational.

## How to Respond to Exclusionary Language

Freezing and speechlessness are common reactions to the shock of exclusionary language. Smiling and laughing are also known responses during uncomfortable encounters. If you feel safe doing so, you can help yourself break out of that silence and inaction by focusing on asking questions.

- "What did you mean by that?"
- "Why do you believe that?"
- "What makes you think that?"
- Or simply: "Would you mind repeating that?"

By asking questions instead of making statements, you can avoid saying something you may regret later on. Sticking to questions can also help you get your bearings. If you are dealing with someone who has more power or privilege, such as a client or supervisor, that may impact your ability to speak freely.

Questions may also signal to them that the interaction needs to slow down. Typically, after a question, the other person will wake up and switch from automatic language mode to conscious language mode. They may backpedal or apologize. Give them a chance to explain. After all, it may be a misunderstanding.

Reclaiming your agency in these moments can be empowering. But please prioritize your own safety and mental health. Reacting with silence or leaving may be the best option. Miss Manners was a big proponent of the thin smile. You can practice your thin smile before leaving.

## How to Apologize

If you made a mistake, wrote or said something regrettable, or were called in or out, remember these three phrases: *You're right. I'm sorry. Thank you.* Feel free to use them individually or in any combination. No need to make it a big deal. No need to make an excuse. No need to make it about yourself. Apologizing can be a vulnerable and uncomfortable act, but having a simple structure can help you take responsibility.

Take care to avoid some common apology pitfalls. In *Say the Right Thing: How to Talk About Identity, Diversity, and Justice*, authors Kenji Yoshino and David Glasgow warn against constructions such as *I'm sorry if* and *I'm sorry but*. To give an effective apology, Yoshino and Glasgow say you need to satisfy the four Rs: recognition, responsibility, remorse, and redress.

**Recognition (no ifpologies):** Couching an apology in *ifs*—*I'm sorry if I hurt you, I'm sorry if you're offended*, or *I'm sorry if you misunderstood me*—makes the reaction the problem. Instead of recognizing the harm, this type of apology construction conveys doubt about the harm. Ifpologies may be common in the most conscious arenas: I have experienced several dharma talks in which the Buddhist teachers—purveyors of mindful speech—offered a nonspecific ifpology to disclaim harmful intentions along the lines of "If we have done anything to cause you harm, we ask for your forgiveness." If actual harm was caused, this type of apology may feel unsatisfying and almost routine. By naming the specific harm without hedging, we can fully recognize and acknowledge the impact of our actions and increase chances of reconciliation.

**Responsibility (no butpologies):** The word *but* often signals a U-turn. In a butpology, saying *I'm sorry but* to blame a circumstance may be perceived as redirecting compassion toward yourself and not taking responsibility. As Yoshino and Glasgow point out, "You not only seek to duck responsibility, but you also suggest the harm could recur. If you say, 'I'm sorry, but I was having a miserable day,' your conversation partner could fairly wonder if you'll repeat your behavior when you have another one." If you blame your words on, say, the interference of medication or mental health, it may help the receiver contextualize your initial gaffe. However, it is unclear whether you are saying that its influence caused you to temporarily forget your true self or caused you to show your true self.

**Remorse (no fauxpologies):** When an apology fails to express remorse, it is a fauxpology. Yoshino and Glasgow describe two main forms of fauxpologizing: underdoing or overdoing the expression of remorse. Underdoing remorse can look like unwillingness to change. Overdoing remorse can look like melodrama and making it about your contrition and how the situation has affected you. In my past, I have tended to overdo my remorse, because I felt so genuinely awful about hurting someone and so obliviously. But what I did not realize was that by saying, "Oh my gods, I can't believe I did that! That's horrible!" I was drawing attention to myself instead of holding space for the person I harmed, all the while appearing to express remorse inauthentically. That's why the phrase *I'm sorry* is usually sufficient.

**Redress (no talkpologies):** Redress is about taking action and changing behavior in addition to saying sorry. Without action, the apology is merely a talkpology. Because many harms accumulate over time, there is no easy formula for redress. Once, after a friend apologized, they immediately asked, "What can I do to fix this? How can we move past this?" While these are skillful questions, I felt rushed. I was not there yet. The first step of redress may be allowing space for others to process their emotions before trying to force a series of actions to wrap it all up. Growth and healing and insight can be supported but not scheduled. So redress is not about easing the apologizer's discomfort. Yoshino and Glasgow describe a few examples of how well-known figures have sought redress: having a series of conversations to listen and learn, spending substantial time learning about a culture, cultivating diversity in their field, combating workplace discrimination, promoting marginalized people and their achievements, and engaging in activism.

The practice of saying *I'm sorry* without diluting it, and by following up with meaningful action, is fundamental to addressing the harm we have caused and strengthening our relationships. If you want to give an in-depth apology, I recommend "The Four Parts of Accountability & How to Give a Genuine Apology," by Mia Mingus.[126]

## When to Say Nothing

Silence may seem like an odd tool for consciousness. But the art of saying nothing can be used to improve relationships, protect privacy, and empower ourselves to be more grounded when we do speak. In other words, saying no words has its own impact.

And as many of us know, silence can take work and focus; it may be challenging to withhold comment. Here are a few situations in which saying nothing may be the most conscious path.

## Listening to Learn

To amplify narratives from firsthand and lived experiences, we need to embrace the art of shutting up so that other voices can be heard. Consider giving people with less privilege the right-of-way in conversation. If you tend to contradict, correct, or question personal accounts that do not conform with your beliefs, you can instead express your surprise by saying, "Thank you, because I learned something new today." When we hold on to thoughts that may disrupt the passing on of knowledge, there's less of a chance we might unintentionally derail or dominate a conversation.

## Protecting Privacy

Outing someone may cause psychological distress, increase their vulnerability to discrimination, or expose them to physical harm. As a general rule, it is safer to assume that outing someone is an invasion of privacy. Avoid mentioning someone's queerness or transness unless you have high confidence that the news is public or can be publicized. Be aware that some people are selectively out, meaning they may be out socially, publicly, and professionally but not out to their families. Some people are out in online forums but not on social media. If someone asks you directly if someone you know is queer or trans, you can tell them to ask that person instead.

Some people make an exception for hypocrites: They consider it fair game to out closeted faith leaders who have preached against queerness, closeted political representatives who have voted for anti-queer legislation, closeted doctors who have practiced "ex-gay" conversion therapy, closeted media personalities who have taunted queer people, and other closeted queer people who have used their positions of influence to trample on queer rights.

Always consider the format, platform, and duration of the content, as well as the consequences of making private information public, screenshot-able, or searchable forever. Avoid divulging, for example, someone's age, sexual orientation, current location, place of residence, or other personal information, especially on social media.

## Minding Your Own Business

For some of us, giving advice is an act of compassion. We reflexively want to reduce suffering. So when people have a problem, we suggest a fix. When people show an interest, we suggest an activity. When people are ill, we suggest a cure. But unwanted advice can cause more distress.

Though this is often gendered as "Men fix, women listen," my own experience contradicts this narrative—women offer advice as often as men do. One consequence of living online is the delusion that our opinions make the world go round. The culture of constantly commenting has trained us to bring this energy of opining to situations where saying nothing is the best option. If itching to offer advice, you can always check in first: *I tried something that worked for me. Let me know if you are interested.*

## Holding Space

We hold space for others by giving them our loving attention, without judging, without trying to fix. I think of holding space as holding energy. When two people — or a room full of people — come together, there is a new energy. Disrupting the energy that was created and contained by the participants can break the hold. Have you ever glanced at something while someone was talking to you? And because you looked away, they stopped talking? Making soft eye contact, keeping your face open or neutral, adopting an aura of patience, and speaking minimally are ways of maintaining the energy.* These behaviors, not coincidentally, are part of listening deeply. We often use our deep-listening skills when we are with our loved ones. But we can also hold space for someone to let them vent and feel understood. Saying nothing and letting their emotion run its course gives us time to think before we do speak.

---

*The twitchy technology of videoconferencing can prevent us from holding space properly. It is harder to get in a groove when we involuntarily speak over one another, and issues with mic muting, frozen video, dropped connections, and other lags and glitches can also throw us off. It almost makes me want to cuddle up with a landline phone.

## CHAPTER FOUR

# PAUSE

Congratulations on making it this far! I hope you are proud of your progress and that you learned something about yourself. In this chapter, I want to take a detour to address some issues that may have come up while exploring the topics in this book. So let's talk about...doubts.

## What-Ifs

It is A-OK to have doubts when using conscious language. Doubt, discomfort, and dissatisfaction can be channeled into creativity. Rather than give up, you can use your doubts to create a means to an end that you can sustain. One person, one message, one style cannot do it all. We need your unique voice and approach.

**What if I don't have time?** Read *The Conscious Language Newsletter.* Join the Conscious Language + Design forum on Facebook. Explore ConsciousStyleGuide.com. And to give yourself some encouragement, try adding the word *yet*: *I don't have time* yet, *so I will make time.*

**What if I can't stick to my plan?** Despite our best intentions, we may fall short, because philosophy is one thing and practice is another. Sometimes it is easy to swap one word for another, present a different perspective, tell a truer story; sometimes there is a mountain of emotions in our path. If you fall short, try changing your expectations. Make goals easier to attain. Design tinier habits. It is important for you to have a win for the sake of morale and longevity. And when you accomplish something, congratulate yourself. Cheer, celebrate, put a note in your win jar. I believe in fanfare (and pie). When we accept the mundaneness of falling short, then forgiving others for falling short can become second nature. Let your practice begin wherever you are.

**What if I say something wrong?** I once hung out with someone who had no problem correcting herself immediately whenever she misspoke. Every time she did, she drew attention to the word she wanted, a more conscious word. Had she chosen the more conscious word from the start, I would have glossed over it. Her generous act of self-correction provided an opportunity for me to examine my own word choices. From that experience, I concluded that we all make mistakes, so we might as well do it skillfully. Let's normalize making mistakes, correcting ourselves, and being transparent.

**What if a word feels inappropriate but nothing else comes to mind?** Do what I do: Either insert *so-called* in front of the word or put the word in quotes. That way, you can use the "wrong" word (just like that) in a way that conveys its iffiness and your lack of endorsement. This approach works best when the word is in a gray area, not when it is widely perceived as volatile.

**What if I can't let go of certain words?** As we awaken to

words and stories that may cause harm, it is important to acknowledge the twinge of grief that can accompany change. When the
mind reaches for words, it is not surprising that we tend to reach
for those with emotional resonance. We have invested more in
*mother* and *father* than *parent*, more in *sister* and *brother* than *sib-
ling*, more in *wife* and *husband* than *spouse*. These words do not
just mean family—they are family. Even wholehearted support
of respectful, compassionate, and mindful terminology may be
accompanied by a feeling of loss.

If you have difficulty breaking up with certain words, try
using them less frequently. Or keep them and move on to an easier shift. Reluctance is not a measure of our goodness or commitment. It is a natural response to change, even when it is our
choice.

**What if no word is ideal?** This is usually the case, but we
manage with what we have. For example, many people of color
dislike the term *people of color*.[1] Reasons include: It's too close to
*colored people*. It erases specific identities. It hints at a solidarity
that does not exist. It enables non-Black people to avoid saying
*Black*. It implies that White people have no color and are the
default. And *people of color* is defined by the boundaries of White-
ness, which keep shifting.* But—it's an improvement over *non-
White*. (Sure, there's *BIPOC*, but nobody much likes that term,
either.) When options are lacking, strive for "reasonable" instead

---

*The White House's Office of Management and Budget is considering a separate cat-
egory for Middle Eastern and North African people, who were previously categorized
as White, which will drastically improve how this group is counted and funded. To
learn more, visit SPD15revision.gov.

of "ideal." Sometimes, un-ideal words, like *people of color*, are the most conscious options.

**What if no one around me uses conscious language?** If you are unable to find others to team up with, learn from, or mutually inspire, try to model conscious language without expecting others to change. Live according to your convictions. Focus on what you can control. Unless doing so is unsafe, practice being your ideal person.

**What if I am overwhelmed by the amount of harmful language?** Becoming more aware of exclusionary language, biased language, and false narratives can be draining. Even those words—*exclusionary, biased, false*—can contribute to numbness. To increase your equanimity in this practice, try practicing detachment. You can, for example, think of non-conscious language as *exclusive style* and conscious language as *inclusive style*. So if you come across an article that excludes nonbinary people, you can note the use of exclusive style as passively as you might note the absence of a serial comma.*

**What if I don't believe in self-censorship?** I mean, gosh, if you put it like that, who would? There are enough pressures imposed upon us, why quash our own freedoms? I get it. But if I may make a suggestion: Instead of conceptualizing the use of conscious language as censoring yourself, reclaim your power. Think of it as saying what you mean. Instead of the oblivious use of exclusionary language, we can guide our words to be in closer alignment with our intentions. And when we can represent

---

*My penchant for the serial comma may be offensive to some people. ¯\\_(ツ)_/¯

ourselves better through conscious language, we reduce the possibility of our words being misconstrued.

**What if I don't care about conscious language?** Then, by all means, don't use it. This book is about conversation, not conversion. (Except for chapter five, Persuade.)

**What if I am happy with the way things are?** Once in a while, see yourself as the villain. Nothing changes if we all think we're the good guy.

### *Key Point*

- If you have doubts, discomfort, or dissatisfaction with conscious language, remember that you are in charge. Create a conscious style that you can sustain and that sustains you.

## Understanding Misalignment

Greater awareness of bias-free language may bring with it a greater awareness of unskillful language used by activists, experts, and marginalized people. An expert on website accessibility might use the gendered term *man-hours*. A nonbinary journalist might misgender their nonbinary colleague. A practitioner of Nonviolent Communication* might conduct a webinar without

---

*Nonviolent Communication (NVC), also known as Compassionate Communication, is a process by Marshall B. Rosenberg, PhD, that involves listening deeply and communicating unmet needs.

accessible captioning. A fat activist might use the term *able-bodied* instead of the preferred term *nondisabled*.

It's a relief, really.

I haven't always felt this way, but I have come to appreciate the complexity of misalignment. I realized that words, like clothes, can be donned and discarded to meet our needs. What we wear may have no ties to our beliefs and intentions. Some words we wear around in public like hats but remove when we get home. Why should any of the conscious language allies in my examples (who are real, by the way) be expected to have deep knowledge of conscious language? It is unrealistic. Disagreeable words, expressions, and narratives do not always reflect the communicator's beliefs. The use of racially insensitive language, for example, is not proof of racist beliefs, nor is the absence of racial slurs evidence of antiracist beliefs.

Other people will not practice conscious language the way you do. And that's OK. Allies come in many forms. If we can foster compassion and forgiveness for one another, then we can make space for perceived deviations or lack of unity.

Here are some reasons people use words that are not aligned with their beliefs.

**Limited attention:** habit, automatic language. In most cases, automatic language serves us well in our busy lives. Paying attention for long periods, like at back-to-back meetings, can be exhausting. Inattentive and sloppy communication between close friends is a form of love and mutual acceptance. It is soothing to drift mindlessly. Not slowing down to weigh and compare words before we talk is usually the default. So when we speak without actively evaluating our words for precision and appropriateness, the likelihood of them not landing well is high. Knowing my tendency toward bluntness, I try to offset automatic language by practicing conscious thinking, so when habit takes over, I do less harm.

**Limited awareness:** limited awareness of history, meaning, or potential impact; limited familiarity; limited proficiency. Use of outdated, offensive, or inappropriate words is often unintentional. Conscious language users who specialize in one field may be less familiar with language use in other fields. Older generations may not have the advantages that younger generations have of being exposed early and frequently to certain terms. Also, people who are multilingual may inadvertently land on the wrong word. For example, speakers of languages without gendered pronouns, such as Mandarin, may accidentally swap *she* and *he* when speaking English.

**Limited ability:** cognitive condition, memory issue, limited clarity, limited focus, illness, overwhelm, intoxication. Physical, emotional, and chemical conditions can alter our ability to think clearly, much less communicate. Emotions, like fear, can make us say things we would not entertain in a calm state. Neurological conditions, like a stroke or Tourette's syndrome, can influence our filters. Illness can turn the most minimal cognitive load into a gigantic task. And many people with memory issues find it challenging to retain what they have learned about preferred and appropriate language. Be aware that many people are dealing with issues that affect their ability to think, remember, and communicate. It would be best to suspend judgment for this reason alone.

**Error:** oversight, typo, mistake, omission, confusion, context error. Mistakes are inevitable, especially when we can't remember if a word is a do or a don't. The contextual nature of conscious language also requires many of us to continually adjust our language, which may produce errors in context-switching. For example, we may become accustomed to the appropriately casual language we use with our local communities and forget to use more careful and precise language in public. In my experience, editors are the most forgiving of errors, because we know how difficult errors are to avoid despite our efforts.

**Documentation:** record, evidence, preservation of history, respect for origins. Historical records can provide evidence for how far we've come. In "A Seat in the Flight Deck: Recognizing and Replacing Biases With Gender Inclusive Language," Emily A. Margolis writes, "There is one notable exception to the gender inclusive language rule—proper names. For example, from its establishment in 1961 through 1973, NASA's Johnson Space Center in Houston, Texas, was known as the Manned Spacecraft Center. Proper names including the adjectives 'manned' and 'unmanned' should not be changed. They are important reminders that, in that moment in time, women were denied the dream of spaceflight."[2]

Documenting language use is crucial in our current fight for equity. The now-defunct Michigan Womyn's Music Festival was open only to "womyn who were born as, and have lived [their] entire life experience as womyn" and had a policy of ejecting festivalgoers who declared themselves to be "transsexual," according to its web page from the year 2000.[3] Though the discriminatory language may be unpleasant to read, it reflects a reality that trans women faced and still face. The archived page also preserves the prior meaning of *transgender(ed)* as a term for cisgender people with stereotype-inconsistent gender expression, a meaning that faded when *transgender* began replacing *transsexual.*

**Strategy:** limited choice, limited resources, experimentation, exploration, space limitations, humor. Language that appears deficient may be so by design. Making language approachable can be the tool we need for connecting people to new ideas. If we start with new ideas, we may alienate potential allies. So there's something to be said for not being too far ahead of the curve. Unless we are patient in building step by step, bridge to bridge, idea to idea, people may not recognize the value of conscious language.

Using a suboptimal word may be necessary when we are short on space or writing copy for SEO (search engine optimization). We can use the term *weather* instead of the appropriate but potentially aggravating term *climate change.*[4] We can call a corporate training session *racial-bias education* instead of *antiracism training* to improve attendance. For an editors' conference, my panelists and I coyly named our talk "Is This Racist?," which we figured was more inviting than "This Is Racist."

While researching language usage on websites and social media feeds, which usually have a progression of content, I often notice the gradual disappearance of specific words over time. (To be clear, I study controversial word use by people in the affected communities, so I'm intentionally searching for these words.) Why haven't the phased-out words been removed if they are potentially offensive? Well, updating takes time, energy, and money—resources that many of us cannot spare. A large organization or well-funded coalition may be able to continually monitor language, vet the recommended alternatives, make informed decisions for each context, post notices on outdated pages, actively maintain old pages, and produce professionally edited content, but expecting an average person, small team, or volunteer-run organization to do the same is unfair and unrealistic.

Cost may be a common factor for the persistence of outdated content. The National Lesbian and Gay Journalists Association (NLGJA) incorporated in 1991 and has since continually evolved its name to be more inclusive, rebranding as *NLGJA: The Association of LGBT Journalists* in 2008, then adding a *Q* in 2013 and a plus sign in 2022. But a legal change to the original name would require an outlay of a quarter million to half a million dollars, according to Ken Miguel, national board president.[5] When an individual or group has a track record of allyship or leadership, consider giving them the benefit of the doubt.

**Disagreement:** experience, expertise, reclamation, competing meanings, competing terminology, competing approaches, competing opinions about impact. What appears to be a misalignment of values may be someone expressing deeper knowledge or coming full circle with their stance. The terminology, use, or pronunciation in question may be, in fact, a highly informed opinion. A similar situation in the editing world is when writers and editors fall prey to zombie rules*—style preferences posing as grammar

---

*Stanford linguistics professor Arnold Zwicky is credited with coining the term *zombie rules*. An example of one is the misguided admonition against split infinitives, as in *to [boldly] go.*

rules. They may think that the flouting of such rules indicates inexperience when it may be the other way around. With conscious language, differences in approach can easily produce different conclusions. Consider appreciating our polylithic complexity and making space for other ways of being conscious.

**Self-protection:** concern, fear of exclusion, mental health, survival. Some people may avoid using specific types of conscious language to protect themselves. A nonbinary person who uses *they/them* pronouns may not feel safe stating them in their work email signature. Even when the work culture appears to be inclusive, individuals on their team or in their department may not be.

Misalignment due to self-protection may describe conscious language advocates who avoid social media for mental health reasons. Social media has provided a platform for activists, advocates, allies, and accomplices to do the invaluable and vulnerable work of educating the wider public about intentional and unintentional acts that marginalize. However, the benefits of learning directly from the source may not be worth the psychological toll of being on social media. The loss of knowledge is often considered an acceptable trade-off for improved health. If you use social media regularly, consider asking yourself if your mental health was better before you began using it.*

Misalignment happens to the most ardent user. Expecting potential allies to comply with an arbitrary linguistic ideal and judging them when they deviate may be giving them too much

---

*Be aware of FOMO, the fear of missing out. If the desire to be on top of the latest words to use or avoid drives your social media use, consider subscribing to advocacy newsletters as a way of managing your time and health.

credit. Doing so assumes that people are in full control of their actions and that they have the power to change, which glosses over differences in ability and resources. Placing too much weight on "wrong" and "right" words may also open the door to terrible self-criticism when we inevitably make mistakes.

By cultivating our compassion for misalignment, we can make peace with words. If we can build up our resilience, then we can more easily work together to change language rooted in disrespect and dominance. Some of you may rightfully balk at the idea that people harmed by words need to make peace with them. Making peace with words does not mean ignoring harmful language or giving up. It means clearing our hearts and minds so that we can counter harmful language with greater ease and greater calm. Making peace with words helps us forgive friends who use the "wrong" speech without shying away from letting them know. We can be less quick to judge the intelligence, political agenda, or wokeness of our colleagues. We can shift our energy and attention to what nurtures us instead of what drains us. We make peace with words so that we can use words to make peace.

## Key Points

- Our words, expressions, and narratives do not always reflect our beliefs.
- Unintentional misalignment may occur due to limited attention, limited awareness, and limited ability. Misalignment can also be intentional due to error, documentation, strategy, disagreement, or self-protection.

- By cultivating our compassion for misalignment, we can make peace with words so that we can use words to make peace.

## Working Across Differences

To work across differences, we need to be open-minded, accommodating, and flexible toward others. Though this concept is usually practiced in a team setting, we can adopt it to work with potential and current allies.

**Calibration involves group modulation.** When disagreements on semantics or word usage or potential offense cause rifts among advocates of conscious language, choosing to calibrate (at least temporarily) may be the key to unity. Often, contentious debates about who's right and who's wrong boil down to lack of calibration—failure to agree on what words mean.

Most of us naturally calibrate with the people we communicate with—we talk how they talk, and they talk how we talk. Calibration is also highly contextual—we can adhere to a style guide, use SEO words for findability, follow communication guidelines at school, respect the rules of a meeting.

How can we communicate in the absence of calibration? One of my biggest advantages in life was growing up with a primary parent who spoke limited English. I had extensive practice in listening beyond words to grasp the intention, regardless of how nonstandard the English was. The charity was mutual. My mother was loving in her accommodation of my limited Mandarin skills. We worked together to communicate as well as we could, a Chinese immigrant and her American daughter.

Communicating in spite of semantic barriers taught me that differences can be bridged through the conscious use of charity, clarification, and collaboration.

**Charity in communication means meeting people where they are.** For the sake of community and fellowship, we can choose to accept communication that is incorrect, imprecise, or inappropriate. For example, we can show charity by forgiving the imperfect apology, the presumptuous question, the use of imprecise terminology. Reading through typos without comment is one type of charity that many of us perform every day. Whether we think people are not conscious enough or too conscious with language, attending to the spirit behind their words can help us keep the conversation moving forward. We can address questionable language later on.

Though anyone can show charity, people of marginalized cultures have borne the responsibility of adopting the language of dominant cultures. To remedy the imbalance, consider calibrating with people of less privilege instead of expecting them to align with you. Forming a new consensus can be a tool for challenging the status quo. If you are uncertain about or unfamiliar with a new-to-you term that more accurately reflects and includes others, consider calibrating to show solidarity. If we expect others to use words that respect us, then for equity, we can do the same for them.

**Clarification or correction in communication is inviting others to meet you where you are.** It is a way to assert or explain uses, especially when charity does not fit the situation.

Modeling is one way of clarifying—simply asserting the desired word or pronunciation by using it. For example, if people talk about *marijuana*, you can participate and use the word *cannabis*. This is an invitation, so model your ideal language without requiring compliance.

Some situations may require more explicit clarification, such as by *calling in* or *calling out* to inform an individual, group, or organization that something they said or did was inappropriate, exclusionary, or discriminatory. With calling in, the clarification is done privately. With calling out, the clarification is done publicly. Some people choose to call out celebrities, corporations, institutions, and others to publicly draw attention to a perceived misstep. However, calling out is best when reserved for entities with a history of failing to respond adequately to abuses. Otherwise, consider giving people the benefit of the doubt. When working across differences, it is preferable to call in and resolve issues on a personal level whenever possible. Note: The gentlest clarification or calling in may unintentionally derail a conversation.

**Collaboration in communication means temporarily meeting people midway.** To enter a collaboration, we can adopt the number-one rule of improvisational theater: using *Yes, and...* Players must say yes to what is happening in the scene and build on it by saying or thinking *Yes, and...* In *Truth in Comedy*, authors Charna Halpern, Del Close, and Kim "Howard" Johnson explain what happens if players do not: "Answering 'Yes, but...' stops any continued growth, while a flat 'No' erases the block that has just been established...Denying the reality that is created on stage ends the progression of the scene, and destroys any chance of achieving a group consciousness."

Within the safety of *Yes, and...*, we can build on ideas for conscious language without negating anyone's contribution. A collaborator may suggest, "Let's use *Brown people* with a capital *B* to be consistent with capital *Black people* and capital *White people* when talking about social groups!" Instead of rejecting the suggestion outright, we can build on it: "Yes, and let's specify which ethnicities we mean by capital *Brown*." When we shoot down imperfect ideas before they've had a chance to be explored, tested, or adapted, we are likely to lose potential allies and, with them, their insights and perspectives. Collaborating for the long term can help build community, curiosity, and confidence. Trials and missteps today inform our direction tomorrow. We cannot edit a blank page.

By being open to other ways of thinking, doing, and being, we can create an inclusive and respectful environment. Instead of passing judgment, try pausing judgment. Of course, when language is intentionally anti-conscious, such as open disparagement of a historically oppressed group, then working together was not a shared goal. But with allies and accomplices, we can choose to forgive, accept, and question unskillful choices. Unless we are confident otherwise, assuming the best in people is a more generous way of responding to what we perceive as unskillful language. And I hope that when I am unskillful, you will be charitable with me too.

### *Key Points*

- Being open-minded, accommodating, and flexible with words will help us build relationships with potential and current allies.

- In order to communicate with one another, we can use several methods. Calibration involves group modulation — choosing to agree on meanings at least temporarily. Charity means meeting people where they are — accepting incorrect, imprecise, or inappropriate language. Clarification or correction is inviting people to meet you where you are — asserting or explaining language. Collaboration is meeting people midway — building on ideas for improving language.

- Assuming the best in people is a more generous way of responding to what we perceive as unskillful language.

## Self-Care

Being considerate of one another's health is the future.

In *World Mental Health Report: Transforming Mental Health for All* (2022), the World Health Organization declared the need for a "worldwide transformation towards better mental health for all." While mental health awareness has increased, the responses to mental health needs have largely been inadequate.

Fortunately, the landscape of mental health support is changing. According to *Fortune*, almost a quarter of workers surveyed by the Harris Poll on its behalf said their employers introduced new mental health services during the Covid-19 pandemic, and over a third said their employers have always offered mental health support.[6]

It is in this spirit that I humbly introduce one of the most effective tools for alleviating stress and distress: Emotional Freedom Techniques. The brevity and efficacy of EFT make it ideal for those who are looking for an alternative or complement to other relaxation methods such as breathwork, movement, and meditation.

This self-care interlude may seem like a misshelved book, but I am seizing this opportunity to help you address any distressful emotions that may arise as you examine your feelings, habits, and beliefs surrounding word and world. Conscious language can transform your relationship with yourself. EFT can help remove emotional blocks that interfere with your practice.

## Emotional Freedom Techniques, or Tapping

Emotional Freedom Techniques can be done in a few minutes and does not cost anything.

I first heard of Emotional Freedom Techniques* in 2010. A friend sent me a link to a video tutorial and said that tapping points on my face can relieve stress. Stress? I have that. But why would tapping my face help? Though I was skeptical, I trusted my

---

*Techniques is plural because EFT is actually a set of tools for relieving distress. In this book, however, I will focus on the main tool.

friend's opinion, so I watched the video. The whole tapping routine took about five minutes. I watched it again, this time following the instructions. The first step was choosing a distressful feeling to work on. I chose one that was small but sharp and lingering. By the end of one round of tapping, I could barely remember what it was. I didn't feel it anymore.

The tapping, it turns out, is on the ends of energy meridians along the body, the same pathways that have been used in acupuncture for at least twenty-three centuries.[7] In traditional Chinese medicine, the meridians are believed to correspond with internal organs. The main precursor to EFT was Thought Field Therapy, founded by Roger Callahan. Callahan's aha moment happened while he was treating a patient who said thinking about water caused "a terrible feeling in the pit of her stomach." He had been studying meridian points, so he asked her to tap on the stomach meridian endpoint below her eye. After a few minutes of tapping, her water phobia was permanently erased.[8] Reading her story reminded me of when I was treated by an acupuncturist for frequent nosebleeds as a child. He inserted a total of two fine needles—one by my nose, the other on my hand. My nosebleeds, which tended to cause embarrassing commotions in school, stopped. So, having grown up with acupuncture and the language of qi, I was open to the concept of tapping on acupuncture points to harmonize the flow of energy.

Kaiser Permanente is among many health institutions that promote the benefits of EFT.[9] A 2022 study on EFT for improving well-being and reducing anxiety among students showed that tapping helped them feel more confident, be more attuned to their emotions, express themselves more appropriately, and achieve a calm emotional state and social connectedness. Furthermore, tapping was "unanimously endorsed" by the teachers and students in the study as an effective technique.

EFT helps you give space and attention to your feelings instead of ignoring them. In everyday life, a prime tapping moment is any in which you feel a disproportionate emotional reaction. You can tap while reading an antagonistic email, decluttering items of sentimental value, feeling anxious before a date, being haunted by a memory, or remembering a past event that is bringing old feelings to the surface. Non-conscious language can cause distress, such as being misgendered by your parents, having your name mispronounced by an instructor, being given unwanted advice by strangers on social media, being subjected to rude comments by passersby, or feeling disrespected by your doctor. When a big or lasting emotional reaction is wholly proportionate to the situation, such as with the death of a family member, you can tap to manage multilayered emotions that arise about your relationship with them.

For readers of this book, tapping moments may also emerge during the development of your framework. Perhaps you have experienced fears such as *I'm afraid I'll say the wrong thing* or *I'm going to be criticized*, resentments such as *You can't say anything anymore* or *Inclusive language has gone too far*, criticisms such as *I just want a list of dos and don'ts* or *The author keeps using words I thought we're supposed to avoid*, or limiting beliefs such as *I won't be able to keep up* or *This will never feel natural to me*. You can tap when people use offensive language and after you have offended someone.

You can tap when you feel unfairly criticized and when you want to criticize another. Tapping on an issue does not mean you are blaming yourself for feeling a certain way. It means taking control when things feel out of control.

Waiting for people to change in order for you to be happy is not a viable option in the long term. Instead, we can empower ourselves — everyone according to their abilities — by tapping on acupuncture points to manage stress. And remember: If you are annoyed, offended, or angered by these suggestions, you can tap on it. In my experience as an EFT practitioner, today's distress is more often than not the emergence of past distress and traumas. It is called Emotional Freedom Techniques because you can use this modality to free yourself of the emotions that hold you back from realizing your potential.

## EFT Tutorial

I became a trained practitioner of EFT in 2011, taught by someone who learned directly from EFT founder Gary Craig. Since then, I have passed the knowledge on to anyone willing to learn. My tutorial is a modified version of Craig's basic protocol based on my experience. EFT does not replace professional medical or mental health support (or your own methods for reducing stress), but it is commonly used in conjunction with other modalities and in partnership with healthcare practitioners. If you prefer to work with a certified EFT practitioner, visit TheTappingSolution .com/eft-practitioners.

# TAPPING POINTS

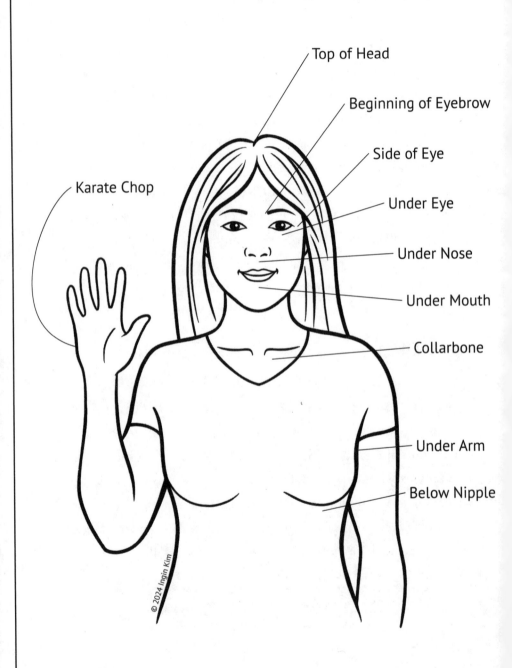

Top of Head

Beginning of Eyebrow

Side of Eye

Under Eye

Under Nose

Under Mouth

Collarbone

Karate Chop

Under Arm

Below Nipple

© 2024 Ingin Kim

### *Tapping points and sequence:*

- Karate Chop: the fleshy edge of your hand
- Top of Head: the crown of your head
- Beginning of Eyebrow: the tip of your eyebrow above your nose
- Side of Eye: the outer corner of your eye on the bone
- Under Eye: under your eye on the bone
- Under Nose: between your nose and your mouth
- Under Mouth: between your mouth and your chin
- Collarbone: one inch below the U-shaped notch at the top of your breastbone (where a necktie knot would be) and one inch to the left or right
- Under Arm: four inches under your armpit (where the wings of a bra would be)
- Below Nipple:* on your ribs, under the chest area

### *Basic protocol:*

**Step 1: Identify the issue.** What is causing your distress? Be specific. Example: *I'm afraid I'll say the wrong thing at work.* If you are not sure, it is OK to start off with a general issue: *I feel bad. I feel anxious. I'm confused. Something just happened.*

**Step 2: Rate the intensity.** How charged is the emotion? Rate the intensity (or take a guess) on a scale from 0 to 10, 10 being the most intense.

**Step 3: Tap and talk.** While tapping on the Karate Chop

---

*This point is often omitted from the basic tapping sequence because some people have trouble accessing it. But if you can tap it, then why not.

point, say the setup statement three times. The standard template is *Even though [issue], I [self-acceptance].*

Example: *Even though I'm afraid I'll say the wrong thing at work, I deeply and completely love myself.* If you find it challenging to say that you love yourself, use another self-acceptance phrase, such as *I want to feel calm, I am doing my best, I am ready to move on, I want to forgive myself, I will try to accept myself, I am willing to consider a new perspective,* or freestyle a phrase of your own.

Then, starting with the Top of Head point, tap about ten times on each point while repeating the words *This issue* or *This feeling* or another short reminder phrase to stay focused.

Variation: While tapping, follow your thoughts. Does the issue recall other events? What was the first or worst time? Tap on aspects that still sting—such as sight, smell, taste, sound, and touch—as you approach the issue from various angles. *I'm going to embarrass myself, like I did in school. I can still hear the kids laughing. I felt so ashamed. It was hard to breathe.*

It is common for your thoughts to change from negative to positive as the emotion lightens. Many people develop deeper insights into their situation and, without forcing it, begin reframing their issues in a more positive light: *Saying the wrong thing at work is an opportunity to learn. Being corrected means my coworkers care. If they stop helping me, it means they've given up. They're trying to help me.*

Or: *If we can't agree on terminology, I can find resources to back up my choices. Maybe I'm wrong, but doing research can help me defend myself at work. If they are wrong, I would be in a better position to educate them.*

Or: *Maybe this job is not right for me. But it's hard to find another job right now. I would rather be here than anywhere else. I've made other things work, because I am strong. I am resourceful. I am adaptable. I can make this work too.*

Reframing happens organically. Just stay connected to your thoughts and feelings as they rise and ebb.

**Step 4: Reassess intensity.** After a round of tapping, take a deep breath. How charged is the emotion now? If the intensity is a 2 or higher, do another round of tapping. Repeat till your intensity ranking is 0 or 1.

Many practitioners tap in sequence, but you can get results by tapping out of sequence or tapping multiple points at once — which can be done with one hand — if you're short on time or in a place not conducive to tapping. You can also tap someone else or be tapped.

For twin points, alternate the tapping (between left and right sides) to incorporate bilateral stimulation. Tapping on twin points simultaneously, or one side only, works too.

More on the setup statement: A setup statement is a negative phrase balanced by a positive phrase. Typically, the negative phrase acknowledges the issue, and the positive phrase expresses self-acceptance. The self-acceptance phrase is not "positive thinking." The statement is designed to address psychological blocks and help you focus on your issue. You can speak the words out loud, mouth them, or think them. Tuning in to the emotion and tapping without using statements or reminders is usually enough for me to clear the distress. But to intensify your focus, it may help to vocalize the statement and reminders if you are able.

## Other Tools

I also recommend two other evidence-based modalities that can support the mental health side of your practice. Though these are not free like EFT, studies show that they are effective in alleviating stress and are well worth considering.

**Neuro Emotional Technique.** NET incorporates the holding of acupressure points to decrease emotional reactivity. According to a 2016 study on the effects of NET on cancer patients with traumatic stress symptoms, "A brief therapeutic course of the NET intervention reduces the reactivity in a number of brain structures associated with the perception of emotional traumas. By reducing the brain's reactivity to traumatic memories, the NET intervention appears to diminish distress associated with such recollections and improve self-regulation."[10]

**Eye Movement Desensitization and Reprocessing.** EMDR can accelerate emotional healing through eye movement or other bilateral stimulation and the use of other therapeutic interventions. According to EMDR.com, "There has been so much research on EMDR therapy that it is now recognized as an effective form of treatment for trauma and other disturbing experiences by organizations such as the American Psychiatric Association, the World Health Organization and the Department of Defense."

Doctors and other certified healthcare practitioners who have undergone training for EFT, NET, or EMDR typically list them on their websites. On Yelp or other websites for location-based, crowd-sourced reviews, you can search for those keywords to locate practitioners near you. If you are curious about learning more about these evidence-based protocols, please research the scientific studies on Google Scholar (https://scholar.google.com).

If you have found other modalities that help you with stress and distress, take the time to create prompts to use them. Taking care of yourself on and off your conscious language journey can create more space for the unknowns ahead.

### *Key Points*

* Being considerate of one another's health is the future.
* Engaging with people and language can cause stress and distress.
* Emotional Freedom Techniques is an effective evidence-based modality for relieving stress and can be used alone, anywhere, for free.

## Words That Inspire Action

When I have reached a plateau, I seek solace in other people's words. Here are some quotations that I hope motivate you as much as they do me.

> "Language is the road map of a culture. It tells you where its people come from and where they are going."
> —Rita Mae Brown, *Starting From Scratch: A Different Kind of Writers' Manual*

"It is not that i am playing word games, it is that the word games are there, being played, and i am calling attention to it."[11]

—Alice E. Molloy, *In Other Words*

"If you have come to help me, you are wasting your time. If you have come because your liberation is bound up with mine, then let us work together."

—Aboriginal activists group Queensland, 1970s*

"Storytelling can be more than a blog post, essay, or book. It can be an emoji, a meme, a selfie, or a tweet. It can become a movement for social change."

—Alice Wong, *Disability Visibility: First-Person Stories From the Twenty-First Century*

"Critics of singular *they* love to think up contexts where it can be awkward or ambiguous, but you can do that with any pronoun, or any word for that matter, and fixing the problem requires rewording, not banning a word outright."

—Dennis Baron, *What's Your Pronoun? Beyond He and She*

"I remember giving a talk and only the boys raised their hands and wanted to be Astronauts. I asked the girls why

---

*This quote is often attributed to Dr. Lilla Watson. According to the Uniting Church in Australia's website, Watson "was not comfortable being credited for something that had been born of a collective process" and preferred the credit used above.

and they said that I said it was the Manned Space Program. That day my language changed and it became the Human Space Program. Language and representation matters."

—Leland Melvin, retired NASA astronaut
(@Astro_Flow, Twitter, August 20, 2018)

"You don't need to start overthinking everything you say or do. That just makes things weird. Disability etiquette isn't about tiptoeing around us and treating us like strange, delicate flowers. (In fact, that's pretty ableist in and of itself.) It's about treating us like full and equal human beings."

—Emily Ladau, *Demystifying Disability:*
*What to Know, What to Say, and How to Be an Ally*

"If a person cannot solve a conflict with a friend, how can they possibly contribute to larger efforts for peace? If we refuse to speak to a friend because we project our anxieties onto an email they wrote, how are we going to welcome refugees, immigrants, and the homeless into our communities? The values required for social repair are the same values required for personal repair."

—Sarah Schulman, *Conflict Is Not Abuse:*
*Overstating Harm, Community Responsibility,*
*and the Duty of Repair*

"If we make ourselves open to the humanity of others *first*, maybe understanding will follow ... What you need, maybe all you need, in fact, is the willingness to love."

—Jennifer Finney Boylan, *Long Black Veil*

"Choose to celebrate this rapid evolution of language because of what it means: that people who have been marginalized for centuries are finding ways of reclaiming agency and legitimacy; that those of us who have been written out of existence are finding ways to rewrite reality to make room for our true selves. The purpose of language is to communicate, not to regulate."

—Alex Kapitan, Radical Copyeditor

## CHAPTER FIVE

# PERSUADE

Apart from modeling the language we want to see and hear more of, what else can we do to create, promote, and cultivate a conscious language culture? One of the challenges some of us may need to overcome is the belief that we are powerless to instigate change. At a conference, a proofreader confessed to me that they believed wholeheartedly in conscious language, but they had no choice but to yield to the higher-level editors. At the proofreading level—where changes are often limited to spelling, punctuation, and grammar—they felt that raising other issues would be crossing the line.

As a former proofreader and longtime rabble-rouser, I saw their situation differently. In their position, they could offer conscious language services and make themself a valuable asset. They could share what they were learning by forwarding news articles or dropping links into the work Slack. They could ask questions to start a conversation or get a feel for their coworkers' or clients' positions. As a freelance editor, I nudged clients by saying, "Hey, Company X is using this terminology / this UX design / this presentation. Do you want to consider it for your company?"

So, if you are in a gatekeeping position, be aware of disempowering yourself. There are many low-risk, low-commitment actions that you can take to shift cultural norms and persuade others to explore conscious language. Plant seeds that get people thinking.

At home, school, and work, as well as in other arenas, communication usually flows in three basic ways: downward, upward, and laterally. Communication by a person at a higher level (usually with more power) to a person at a lower level (usually with less power) travels downward. Upward communication would be the opposite. Lateral communication occurs between people of equal rank (symmetrical power). Your relationship to your audience can help you determine the action you can take.

If the communication is downward—parent to child, teacher to student, supervisor to worker—the persuader can establish an ideal style, take steps to create an inclusive culture, and delegate. Rules that come from the top can be equitable and fair when upward feedback is welcomed and a diversity of voices are involved in the decision-making. (For resources on using conscious language with children, visit ConsciousStyleGuide.com /teaching-children.)

If the communication is upward—child to parent, student to teacher, worker to supervisor—the persuader can introduce topics, ask questions, raise concerns, make suggestions. A teen can make their parent aware of outdated language. A student can inform their teacher about their culture. A worker can ask their supervisor about website accessibility. If you have more influence and latitude than other potential persuaders, consider "stepping up" if they are not in a position to tolerate pushback.

And if the communication is lateral, between people in similar positions, the persuader can invite collaboration on decisions and actions.

## Getting People on Board

To get buy-in on a change to a word, style, guide, policy, or culture from any group at any level:

**Step 1: Identify the influencers.** Who has the power to act on or amplify appeals for change, either downward or upward? At home, both the children and the adults have influence. At school, both the students and faculty have influence. At work, anyone who makes decisions has influence.

**Step 2: Identify potential allies.** You may want to begin where you have allies or folks interested in change. Acting as a group, especially one that is broad and diverse, can encourage others to join in.

**Step 3: Create the conditions for minds to change.** Demanding compliance, making people feel bad, and instilling fear does not change minds. In fact, proselytizing or pressuring people may turn them off to ideas they would otherwise support. We need to give people space to process, which will help them be open to change. "Telling people they're racist, sexist, and xenophobic is going to get you exactly nowhere," said Alana Conner while executive director of Stanford University's Center for Social

Psychological Answers to Real-World Questions. "It's such a threatening message. One of the things we know from social psychology is when people feel threatened, they can't change, they can't listen."[1] Instead, create the conditions that make it safe for people to change their minds. This may mean having a private conversation with no distractions and being conscious of your intonation, inflection, and nonverbal communication.

**Step 4: Appeal to people's interests.** In addition to providing a nonjudgmental setting, focus on benefits and appeal to people's interests. Ask yourself: *What do they care about? What matters most to them? What's in it for them?* When trying to persuade someone, it is essential to frame your proposition from their perspective. To minimize potential overwhelm, focus on simple objectives, such as reviewing gendered language, if conscious language as a whole may cause them to freeze up. (For ideas on dividing conscious language into smaller parts, see chapter two's "Exploring Your Interests" on page 49.)

Here are some examples of appeals to personal, social, or corporate interests. Please adapt these templates for your context. To increase effectiveness, be specific whenever possible:

- **Accuracy.** "By using accurate and precise terminology, we can avoid making assumptions and reduce the risk of misunderstandings."
- **Respect.** "By respecting people's names, personal pronouns, and identity labels, we can build trust, loyalty, and rapport."
- **Safety.** "By embracing socially conscious language, we can

send a strong message that people will feel seen, heard, and valued."

- **Optics.** "By adopting inclusive terminology, we can signal our commitment to diversity, equity, and inclusion and avoid the perception that we are uncaring or behind the times."
- **Professionalism.** "By updating our terminology, we can communicate ideas in a more professional and appealing manner."
- **Logic.** "By changing exclusionary narratives, we can align our actions with our diversity and inclusion mission."
- **Popularity (of specific uses).** "By using bias-free terminology, we will be in sync with [admired person, group, organization, publication]." (Tip: To provide evidence of mainstream adoption, you can perform a site-specific search on Google.com for inclusive terminology. For example, to search the *New York Times* website for the word *queer,* use *site:nytimes.com queer.*)
- **Flexibility.** "By learning about conscious language, we can increase our options for communication and empower our team members to adapt it to their personal needs and styles."
- **Simplicity.** "By adhering to an existing style publication, such as one on ConsciousStyleGuide.com/general, we can make decisions more quickly, easily, and consistently without having to create our own guide."
- **Community.** "By using language that prioritizes collaboration, morale, and mental health, people with diverse

backgrounds can appreciate one another's differences and thrive as a group."

- **Bottom line.** "By using inclusive terminology, we can enhance our brand or reputation, connect with and retain a wider audience, attract customers who align with socially conscious beliefs, and avoid losing customers to the competition."
- **Laws.** "By designing for accessibility, we can help our business meet or exceed any legal requirements." (Website accessibility lawsuits were 37 percent of the ADA Title III lawsuits filed in federal court in 2022.)[2]
- **Freedom.** "By using language that includes, respects, and empowers, we can advocate freedom and choice for more of us."

**Step 5: Address their blocks.** The most direct way of addressing people's blocks to action is to suss out the answers to these questions: *What keeps them from adopting this terminology? What about their current terminology appeals to them? What do they need in order to consider this direction?* If possible, ask them directly. Then use the answer to streamline and focus your efforts.

**Step 6: Make it easy.** Meet low motivation with low-effort learning. At work, you can create a style sheet for easy reference. (See "Creating a Style Sheet" on page 239.) If people are not using the style sheet, bring style to them: Create a #Style channel on Slack, Discord, Microsoft Teams, or other platforms where people can share questions and ideas. Send style notifications by email. (Make sure the recipients have opted in and you are not spamming them.) What other barriers to learning can you remove?

When suggesting changes to terminology, avoid devolving into an argument about intention or definition. Arguing about intention will likely be frustrating and fruitless. To minimize harm, we need to orient ourselves to what language does, not what we hope it will do. Disagreement over definitions is a sign of incommensurability—a failure to calibrate on the ground floor. When minds are unable to meet because, for example, one person believes that *woman* is a biological concept and another insists that *woman* is a social concept, then conversations wilt before they can bloom. Instead, focus on the impact of language. How might our language affect people? Regardless of intention or definition, what is the impact on equity and freedom?

Remember, getting buy-in is not limited to upward, employee-to-supervisor communication. You can use these approaches to persuade people at all levels. Depending on your audience, a particular format or platform may be more effective. When dealing with people who are resistant, you may need to read their tone and body language to determine the ideal moment to present an idea.

### *Key Points*

- First, believe in your power to create change.
- To persuade others to consider using language more consciously, you can create conditions for minds to change. People who feel threatened are unlikely to listen.

- Craft a proposition that appeals to your audience's interests. Address their psychological blocks, and make it as easy as possible for them to take action.
- Avoid arguing about intention or definition. Focus on the impact of the language, how it affects people.

## Building a Ref Stack

What is a ref stack? *Ref stack* is a term I borrowed from *tech stack*, the stack of tools, languages, and technologies used to build a software application. Pondering language can be an endless abstraction, but building a stack of go-to reference works can help ground and orient you.* References are not the be-all, end-all, but many arguments about style or definition can be nipped in the bud when everyone agrees on an authority.

Answers to many of your conscious language questions can be found in existing resources, many of them free and accessible online. In this section, I share some of my favorite reference works. Please consider this a beginning point to help you build your own ref stack. It is not intended to be a comprehensive or exhaustive list. I hope that looking through the range of styles will provide ideas for exploring your own and deciding whether you want to specialize in specific areas or be a generalist like me.

Building your ref stack can help you clarify your scope. Having concrete guidance, definitions, and standards in front of you will give you something to question, criticize, and compare your

---

*ConsciousStyleGuide.com can be described as a digital ref stack.

beliefs against. We do not know how well a pair of pants will fit till we put it on. And reference works, starting with the table of contents, can prompt ideas for your scope.

Choosing reference works can be daunting when you are unfamiliar with the topic. A quick method is to open one—any one—and find a common entry word that is meaningful to you. Once you've picked a word, check the entry in another reference. (I check *bisexual*, *gender*, and *sex*. Because their meanings have shifted during my lifetime, I can use them to gauge how useful a resource will be to me.) This is your litmus test. Repeat this as many times as is helpful. One resource should rise to the fore, but if none does, open a couple more. Spending time comparing reference works will save you time later. A resource that meets you where you are or inspires you to change your thinking is the ideal resource for you. One that does not resonate will eventually hinder instead of help, so it is important to be realistic about where you are so you can lean on resources within a few degrees of how you work and think.

There's no need to stick with just one resource per topic—after all, ref stacks adapt to the user—but selecting a go-to resource can free up mental space for other decisions and make it easier to coordinate style with a team or client. Instead of giving three resources on the same topic equal weight, designate one as the primary resource, the others as the secondary and tertiary resources. If what you need is not in the main one, move on to the next in line. This system also encourages polylithic thinking, because style guides contradict one another—there is no one correct way. Once you become more familiar with the topics, you can build on your framework by adding to your ref stack.

Ref stack possibilities are endless, so I recommend building selectively and getting to know each resource. Familiarizing yourself with a reference work can be as minimal as reading the front matter (instead of skipping it like you usually do) and the table of contents. Most reference works tell you how to use them, what you can look up, and which other references they recommend. References are there for you to refer to, so memorization is not necessary. In "Creating a Style Sheet" on page 239, I share tips for making your own style sheet, where you can organize links to ref stacks for easy reference. (Find this list on ConsciousStyleGuide.com/refstack.)

## Dictionaries

For your ref stack, pick a dictionary (or several) based on its strengths, such as scope, usability, and relevance. Dictionaries have their own internal processes for monitoring, researching, and accepting new terms, so faster inclusion of not-yet-mainstream words, like *Latine* and *demigirl/demiboy*, does not make a dictionary more objectively relevant. Dictionaries that identify offensive or pejorative words can be a logical first resource when trying to determine appropriate usage. Because dictionaries are records of usage, comparing definitions across dictionaries helps you gain a fuller picture of where we are and where we have been.

Be aware that exclusion from a mainstream dictionary does

not undermine a word's legitimacy. Modern English dictionaries are descriptive, not prescriptive—that is, they record, not prescribe, how words are used. Countless words are omitted due to lack of popular use, lack of adequate citations, lack of space, lack of need for a definition, or lack of occurrence in nonspecialized contexts. New additions may have escaped your notice—like *Latinx* (*American Heritage Dictionary* online, circa 2017) and the pronoun *ze* (*Oxford English Dictionary*, 2018). Some words in wide use get stuck at the gate, like *fuck* was from 1795 to 1965.[3] Most slang, a nonconforming register spontaneously birthed within subcultures, is challenging to categorize. If a word has currency, then it is a real word.

My go-to online dictionaries include:

- *Merriam-Webster* (https://merriam-webster.com or https://m-w.com)
- YourDictionary (https://www.yourdictionary.com)
- Dictionary.com

## Style Guides

A style guide, which can be a tome or a memo, in print or online, is a collection of guidelines on such matters as terminology, spelling, possessives, punctuation, capitalization, numbers, abbreviations, and formatting. Because your style will refer to other styles, it helps to know how guides work, so please bear with me.

With the help of a style guide, we can more easily present a cohesive, consistent, and comprehensible experience for our audiences. Other types of guidance can be included to support the guide's purpose and the audience's goals, like grammar or technology tips. Editors often create style sheets for each project to track the above and more.

Style guides are typically created with a specific purpose for a specific community. Most guides are created for internal use, like corporate identity guides or editorial style guides. Of these, a few are published in print or online. A few guides created for specific communities have gained an audience beyond the original reach, such as *The Associated Press Stylebook* and *The Chicago Manual of Style*. Some guides are created by a specific community for users outside the community and can be presented as topical guides or press releases tied to recent events. Most style guides listed on ConsciousStyleGuide.com are examples of this type: guidance created by and about a marginalized community for journalists.

Guides that are current, address a broad and diverse audience, and cover inclusive or conscious language will be the most useful to start with. These often include media guides for use in publishing and journalism but may also be guides created for marketing, psychology, education, and nonprofits. Any guide can be used with the understanding that outside of the stated purpose and context, the advice may not be appropriate.

Broadly speaking, mainstream style guides serve a mainstream audience. For opinions on terminology that has not reached a critical mass, check style guides created by community coalitions or activists.

## Terminology-Based Guidance

Guides consisting of word lists or databases can provide immediate answers. Usually intended for use in specific contexts, they allow quick-and-dirty lookups for people whose objectives are aligned with theirs.

- The Diversity Style Guide (https://www.diversitystyle guide.com/)
- "Unspinning the Spin," by the Women's Media Center (https://womensmediacenter.com/unspinning-the-spin/)
- "BuzzFeed Style Guide"* (https://www.buzzfeed.com/buzz feednews/buzzfeed-style-guide)
- *The Associated Press Stylebook* (fee) (https://apstylebook.com/)

## Guidance by Topic

To avoid duplicating the resources on ConsciousStyleGuide.com, I've selected a few style guides to demonstrate the range of information available.

### *Ability and disability:*
- "Disability Language Style Guide," by the National Center on Disability and Journalism (https://ncdj.org/style -guide/)

---

*\*BuzzFeed News* shut down in May 2023, but the online style guide can be used as a record of web- and social media–related language.

### Age:

- "Guidelines for Age-Inclusive Communication," by Changing the Narrative (https://changingthenarrativeco.org/age-inclusive-communication/)

### Appearance:

- "How Should a Health Brand Talk About Weight?," by *Self* (https://www.self.com/story/self-weight-health-style-guide)

### Criminal justice:

- "The Language Project," by the Marshall Project (https://www.themarshallproject.org/2021/04/12/the-language-project)

### Ethnicity, race, and nationality:

- *Cultural Competence Handbook*, by the National Association of Hispanic Journalists (find on https://nahj.org/resource-center/)
- "How to Talk About Native Nations: A Guide," by Native Governance Center (https://nativegov.org/resources/how-to-talk-about-native-nations/)
- "NABJ Style Guide," by the National Association of Black Journalists (https://nabjonline.org/news-media-center/styleguide/)

### Gender, sex, and sexuality:

- "GLAAD Media Reference Guide," by GLAAD (https://www.glaad.org/reference)

- "Stylebook and Coverage Guide," by the Trans Journalists Association (https://styleguide.transjournalists.org/)

### Health:
- "ACOG Guide to Language and Abortion," by the American College of Obstetricians and Gynecologists (https://www.acog.org/contact/media-center/abortion-language-guide)

### Plain language:
- "Free Guides," by the Plain English Campaign (https://www.plainenglish.co.uk/free-guides.html)

### Spirituality, religion, and atheism:
- "Antisemitism Uncovered: A Guide to Old Myths in a New Era," by the Anti-Defamation League (https://antisemitism.adl.org/)
- "Muslim Media Toolkit: Shifting the Narrative," by Tasmiha Khan (https://rjionline.org/news/muslim-media-toolkit/)
- "What Is Atheism?," by American Atheists (https://www.atheists.org/activism/resources/about-atheism/)

## Guidance by Context

Some language guides promote inclusion, diversity, equity, and/or access within a specific context, such as a company, profession, field, or industry. Find organizational websites and publications in your area, and observe their language. Here are a few examples.

**Arts and humanities:**

- "Describing Visual Resources Toolkit," by the University of Michigan Library (https://describingvisualresources.org/)

**Chemistry:**

- "ACS Inclusivity Style Guide," by the American Chemical Society (https://www.acs.org/content/acs/en/about/diversity/inclusivity-style-guide.html)

**Education:**

- "Statement on Gender and Language," by the National Council of Teachers of English (https://ncte.org/statement/genderfairuseoflang/)

**Finance:**

- "The A to Z of Financial Terms," by the Plain English Campaign (find on https://www.plainenglish.co.uk/free-guides.html)

**Health:**

- "Guidelines" (for communication on suicide, mental health, and drugs) by Mindframe (https://mindframe.org.au/guidelines)

**Healthcare:**

- "Advancing Health Equity: A Guide to Language, Narrative and Concepts," by the American Medical Association

(https://www.ama-assn.org/about/ama-center-health
-equity/advancing-health-equity-guide-language-narrative
-and-concepts-0)

## History:

- "A Guide to Conscious Editing at Wilson Special Collections Library," by the University of North Carolina at Chapel Hill University Libraries, 1st ed. (find on https://cdr.lib.unc.edu/concern/articles/qv33s598j)

## Journalism:

- "Dart Style Guide for Trauma-Informed Journalism," by the Dart Center (https://dartcenter.org/resources/dart-center-style-guide)

## Law:

- "Gender Diversity in Legal Writing: Pronouns, Honorifics, and Gender-Inclusive Techniques," by the British Columbia Law Institute (find on https://www.bcli.org/project/gender-diversity-in-legal-writing-honorifics-pronouns-and-gender-inclusive-techniques/)

## Museums:

- "Family Inclusive Language Chart," by Margaret Middleton (find on https://www.margaretmiddleton.com/resources)

*Philosophy:*
- "Guidelines for Non-Sexist Use of Language," by the American Philosophical Association's National Committee on the Status of Women in the Profession (https://www.apaonline.org/page/nonsexist)

*Psychology:*
- "Inclusive Language Guide," by the American Psychological Association (https://www.apa.org/about/apa/equity -diversity-inclusion/language-guidelines)

*Publishing:*
- *The Chicago Manual of Style* (fee) (https://www.chicago manualofstyle.org/)

*Technology:*
- "Inclusive Terminology," *W3C Manual of Style*, by W3C (https://w3c.github.io/manual-of-style/#inclusive)

## Thesauruses

Thesauruses are a good source for word alternatives, but beware: They may show words that are inappropriate. Use your judgment for your context or develop the context needed to support prima facie inappropriate words.

- WordHippo (https://wordhippo.com/)
- Thesaurus.com (https://www.thesaurus.com/)

## Newsletters

My one-of-a-kind newsletter rounds up the latest opinions, observations, and news about conscious language.

- *The Conscious Language Newsletter,* by Karen Yin (https://consciousstyleguide.com/newsletters)

## Discussion Forums

Thanks to the generosity of strangers in forums, it is easier than ever to hop online, ask questions, share information, and engage in conversation. The range of perspectives in forums is their strength.

- Conscious Language + Design (private Facebook group), by Karen Yin (https://www.facebook.com/groups/consciouslanguage)

## Other Resources

Your ref stack can include reference works, writers, and writings you trust, even if they do not directly address conscious language issues. Factual references and verification tools enable accuracy— a primary conscious language concern—and include atlases, almanacs, encyclopedias, biographical dictionaries, geographical references, and books of quotations. To portray your own or different cultures, communities, professions, and hobbies with accuracy and believability, consider adding trade publications, topical guides, and bilingual, slang, or regional English dictionaries to your ref stack. Resources and contact information for editors, beta readers, and cultural consultants would go in your ref stack too.

### Writing and editing:

- "Copyeditors' Knowledge Base: Editing Tools," by Katharine O'Moore-Klopf (http://kokedit.com/ckb_4.php)
- "SPJ Toolbox," by the Society of Professional Journalists (https://www.journaliststoolbox.org/)
- "Writer Things," by Karen Yin (https://karenyin.com/writer-things/)
- Mythcreants (https://mythcreants.com/)
- TV Tropes (https://tvtropes.org/)
- Writing With Color (https://writingwithcolor.tumblr.com/)

### Verification tools:

- "How to Research a Quotation," by the New York Public Library (https://www.nypl.org/blog/2013/11/22/how-to-research-quotations)
- "Verification Toolbox," by First Draft (https://firstdraftnews.org/verification-toolbox/)

### Consultants:

- Editors of Color Database, by Karen Yin (https://editorsofcolor.com/database/)
- Diverse Databases, by Karen Yin (http://diversedatabases.com)

## *Key Points*

- Building a stack of go-to reference works can help ground and orient you.
- Having concrete guidance, definitions, and standards in front of you will give you something to question, criticize, and compare your beliefs against.

# Creating a Style Sheet

Now that you have diverse sources of information, it is time to add something of your own: your personal style sheet. The purpose of a style sheet is to help you be consistent, anticipate issues, and save time. Ideally, it addresses issues well in advance of a deadline or other style emergency.

# Setting Up Your Style Sheet

Style specifically for conscious language can be organized by terminology, topic, type, or a combination.

- Style sheets arranged by terminology are alphabetized. This is the least complicated way to manage entries but can become unwieldy. To avoid duplicating explanations, one entry can refer to another.
- Style sheets arranged by topic can help you locate style that affects a specific group. The topics listed under "Guidance

by Topic" on page 231 are based on topics on Conscious StyleGuide.com.

- Style sheets arranged by type—like terminology, abbreviations, punctuation, and slang—can reveal patterns in your preferences and increase appreciation for consistent inconsistencies.

Style sheets can feature global instructions, such as reminders to consider context and contextualization. Keep these bulleted notes at the top of your sheet.

## Supplementing Another Style Guide

If your personal style sheet supplements a major style guide, establish the order of consultation. As a supplement, your style sheet will note deviations from the major style guide, using its headings. Because it is a list of extras and exceptions, when you have a style question, your style sheet takes precedence. Typically, the major style guide comes next, and then that style guide's official dictionary. If they do not provide adequate guidance on the conscious language topic you need, prioritize another resource that does.

If you are supplementing a corporate style guide, you can either insert a separate section on conscious language or splice in notes throughout. It may be easier to establish macro rules and note the exceptions rather than make micro decisions.

## Reviewing the Style Sheet

If your intention is to stay current, you may want to research words and phrases from scratch every time a style question comes up, because change happens. However, this level of rigor may not be necessary for the average user of conscious language. The frequency will depend on your needs, abilities, and resources.

- If you use your style sheet for school or work, institute regular and methodical review of the content.
- If you work with a team, the review can involve a submission system and feedback. For any size company, establishing an explicit policy can help you avoid making piecemeal decisions, which typically lack cohesion and a clear intention. How much and what type of input do you require for making a change to the style sheet? If you codified your reasoning in a policy, what would it say? Will the change affect existing materials or only content going forward? Do you need a budget?
- If you represent a business entity in the public eye, you can be transparent about the review process in order to build trust and credibility.
- If your style sheet is yours alone, and nobody else refers to it, then make it comprehensible for your future self, who may need more notes.

When you indicate your preferences in your style sheet, it may be helpful to include a date. Your attitudes are likely to evolve, and your framework is likely to change. Your notes are a journal of your quandaries and solutions.

## *Key Points*

- A personal style sheet helps you be consistent, anticipate issues, and save time.
- Your personal style sheet can consist of style notes as well as a journal of your quandaries and solutions.
- For ref stack ideas, visit ConsciousStyleGuide.com.

# FINAL THOUGHTS

Imagine a world in which every need for nourishment, community, security, and safety is met. Where all beings are valued and have a voice. Our resources are abundant, our opportunities equitable. The institutions supporting us—housing, healthcare, education, transportation—do not forget or disable anyone. The governance handles conflicts with fairness and integrity, and a culture of generosity and forgiveness permeates all interactions. In short, a world in which no one is oppressed.

In such a utopia, can language offend or injure? When oppression does not exist, would anyone argue about words?

While I believe that humans will argue about anything, I also believe that much of our discontent with language is in response to chronic injustice and disempowerment. If we could directly change the systems and institutions that maintain a power imbalance, then we may have less of a need to fiddle with words. But most of us cannot create change at higher levels. Few have the power to decide who is allowed to use their voice, whose customs and belief systems dominate, whose perspective becomes *the* perspective, whose language becomes the default, who can name and label, who gets credit and compensation, what is

THE CONSCIOUS STYLE GUIDE

criminalized, which unions are legitimate, what is civil, what is proper, what is taboo, what is beautiful, who owns land, who lives where, who gets access, who has rights, who writes history. So to fight for our basic freedoms, we try to create change through words.

The greater our awareness of what has transpired in the past, the better our understanding of the present. Ethnic pride used to bewilder me. I found it difficult to understand how anyone could be proud of something they did not achieve. But now I have a different take. Chinese American pride, for example, exists precisely because of history. It is the backdrop of anti-Chinese immigration laws, citizenship bans, violence, taxation, propaganda, erasure of Chinese people's deep roots in the US, and otherizing in mass media and literature that makes Chinese American pride a revolutionary act. Though we cannot change the past, we can change our future by contextualizing our present. By using words and stories that reflect reality and possibility, we can minimize harmful patterns. But we do not have this option if we do not know how to use language consciously.

I disagree with one of the touchstones of mainstream style — the imperative to not "contort" language, because it may be distracting for the audience. Sometimes, contortions are the most ideal way to introduce a new, inclusive concept, so long as there is a contextual bridge. Readers who are distracted by conscious language, such as the singular *they/them*, may need time to get accustomed to it. The conscious response is not the avoidance of unfamiliar language but the more frequent use of it. Each moment of unfamiliarity, even discomfort, is a teachable moment or window—an opportunity to interrupt automatic language and introduce more equitable ways of thinking. Lack of familiarity should not dictate what words we can use for equity. Let's normalize building bridges to comprehension and creating context that meets readers at the gate. Also, we contort language all the time—to sell ideas and products, to assert a viewpoint through jargon, to soften violence through euphemisms. Why not consciously contort for the sake of freedom and connection? Communicating requires us to make choices, and every choice is an opportunity to include, respect, and empower.

My personal conscious language style stemmed from my editorial style, which evolved through decades of working closely with, listening to, and accommodating a diverse group of people and personalities in a wide range of conditions, and it continued to evolve while I wrote this book. If I could snap my fingers and make everyone adopt my conscious language practice, I would refuse. What a tremendous loss of intellectual, philosophical, and spiritual diversity that would be.

To end, I leave you with a few thoughts on conscious discernment. Why discernment? To me, conscious language is about having the skills to discern between often-conflated concepts in order to clear a path. As with the rest of this book, my intention is not to elicit agreement but to provide a draft for you to revise.

As you explore conscious language, practice discerning between the following:

- intention and impact
- offense and harm

- individual and group
- out-group and in-group
- tokenizing and welcoming
- lip service and commitment
- calling in and calling out
- malice and misaligned words
- temporary indecision and chronic inaction
- inappropriate content and inadequate context
- broad terms that include and broad terms that erase
- short-term impacts and long-term impacts
- talking about people and talking to people
- making space and taking up space

Equity is not a single destination but infinite points along infinite paths. Let us not hide from the inevitable discomfort that comes with the work of strengthening connections, of seeking to understand and be understood. To rebuild, we must have the patience for the noise and mess of construction. The pain of the most civil disagreement, the pain of well-intended but unkind words, the pain of incommensurable worldviews—that is all part of not just using conscious language but life.

# ACKNOWLEDGMENTS

Without hesitation, I thank my sharp-as-heck agent, Laurie Abke-meier. You are the best advocate a writer could hope for.

To Tracy Behar, my brilliant editor and publisher, thank you for believing in me and my vision. It is an honor to have the most important book of my life be published by you. Many thanks to your patient and hardworking team at Little, Brown Spark for helping to bring this book into existence.

This book would be less comprehensible and comprehensive — and just less — if it weren't for my awesome readers. Thank you, Teresa Conrow, Tien Nguyen, Eric Wat, Michael McDunnah, Sydnee Thompson, Dee Hudson, Mey Rude, and Carol Yin. There is a part of each of you within these pages.

A heartfelt and long overdue thank-you to my Conscious Style Guide advisory council for answering my questions no matter how random: Alice Y. Hom, Steve Bien-Aimé, Henry Fuhrmann, Christine Ma, and Steve Kleinedler. Henry, you left us too soon, but your contributions to conscious language continue to change the world.

Many thanks to Dawn McIlvain Stahl, social media manager extraordinaire, for crafting posts on behalf of Conscious Style Guide; Katharine O'Moore-Klopf, Mark Allen, Erin Brenner, and

Sylvia Sukop for all the ways you've supported my career; Sara Ryan for using your librarian powers to help me with my proposal; Larry Yang for your prayer of aspiration; and Wisdom Publications for permission to publish it.

Words cannot capture the love and appreciation I have for my die-hard cheerleaders. In addition to those named above, I thank Lee Ann Goya, Diep Tran, Christine Eghenian, Helene Pauly, Shay Fan, Maggie Lauren Brown, Elia Ben-Ari, Carol Kim, and Shirin Shamsi. To Mama, 我愛妳. 謝謝你生下我. To Ingin Kim, my favorite beta reader, thank you for making life delightful.

Last but not least, I am enormously grateful to the countless many whose intellectual generosity helped to shape my philosophy of language and life. In that group, I include writers of norm-questioning discourse, didactic activists on social media, participants in online editing or writing communities, my beloved intentional community at the Johnston Center for Integrative Studies program at the University of Redlands, and the many official and unofficial teachers who had a hand in expanding my consciousness.

Thank you all for giving me the courage to give birth to this book.

# NOTES

**Before You Begin**

1. Thich Nhat Hanh, *The Art of Communicating* (HarperOne, 2013), 55.

**Chapter One:** *Prepare*

1. "You Shall Know a Word by the Company It Keeps," Quote Investigator, September 18, 2022, https://quoteinvestigator.com/2022/09/18/word -company/.
2. Matthew Nussbaum, "Trump Leans on Inflammatory Rhetoric to Defend Border Separation," *Politico*, June 19, 2018, https://www.politico .com/story/2018/06/19/trump-border-children-inflammatory-rhetoric -655479.
3. "Governor Huckabee Makes His First Blaze Appearance," BlazeTV, November 16, 2015, https://youtu.be/p0mv66pFkU0.
4. John Parkinson, "Steve King's 'Racist' Immigration Talk Prompts Calls for Congressional Censure Amid Border Wall Fight With Trump," ABC News, November 30, 2018, https://abcnews.go.com/Politics/steve-kings -racist-immigration-talk-prompts-calls-congressional/story?id=59513584.
5. Alexandra Topping, "Morrissey Reignites Racism Row by Calling Chinese a 'Subspecies,'" *The Guardian*, September 3, 2010, https://www .theguardian.com/music/2010/sep/03/morrissey-china-subspecies-racism.
6. Jen Yamato, "The Coen Brothers: 'The Oscars Are Not That Important,'" *Daily Beast*, updated July 12, 2017, https://www.thedailybeast.com/the -coen-brothers-the-oscars-are-not-that-important.
7. Dominique Mosbergen, "Border Patrol Agent Admits to Intentionally Hitting Migrant With Truck," *HuffPost*, August 13, 2019, https://www .huffpost.com/entry/arizona-border-patrol-agent-matthew-bowen -pleads-guilty_n_5d526bc8e4b0cfeed1a293e2.
8. Morgan Godvin and Charlotte West, "The Words Journalists Use Often Reduce Humans to the Crimes They Commit. But That's Changing,"

Poynter, December 15, 2020, https://www.poynter.org/reporting-editing /2020/the-words-journalists-use-often-reduce-humans-to-the-crimes -they-commit-but-thats-changing/.

9. Amy Anderson, "Brain Health: Changing the State of Mental Health Education and Stigma," Yale School of Medicine, October 12, 2021, https://medicine.yale.edu/news-article/brain-health-changing-the-state -of-mental-health-education-and-stigma/.

10. Diane Petrella, "Do You Want to Lose Weight…or Release Weight?," updated August 9, 2021, https://dianepetrella.com/blog/self-talk/do-you -want-to-lose-weight-or-release-weight/.

11. Ian McMahan, "Do You Think of Yourself as an Athlete or an Exerciser? Here's Why It Matters," *The Washington Post*, February 22, 2022, https:// www.washingtonpost.com/wellness/2022/02/22/athlete-definition -exerciser-difference/.

12. Henry Goldblatt, "A Brief History of 'Karen,'" *The New York Times*, updated August 3, 2020, https://www.nytimes.com/2020/07/31/style /karen-name-meme-history.html.

13. Nancy Coleman, "Why We're Capitalizing Black," *The New York Times*, July 5, 2020, https://www.nytimes.com/2020/07/05/insider/capitalized -black.html.

14. Robert Hudson, ed., *The Christian Writer's Manual of Style* (Zondervan, 2004), 170.

**Chapter Two: *Plan***

1. "Understanding Implicit Bias," Kirwan Institute for the Study of Race and Ethnicity, archived October 27, 2020, at the Wayback Machine, https://web.archive.org/web/20201027025919/http://kirwaninstitute .osu.edu/research/understanding-implicit-bias/.

2. "Epilepsy Terminology on Facebook," Epilepsy Society, November 3, 2015, https://epilepsysociety.org.uk/blog/epilepsy-terminology-facebook.

3. "Fact Check: The Word Picnic Does Not Originate From Racist Lynch- ings," Reuters, July 13, 2020, https://www.reuters.com/article/uk-factcheck -picnic-origin-lynchings-idUSKCN24E21V.

4. Franklin Hughes, "Lynching Picnic," Jim Crow Museum, July 2021, https://jimcrowmuseum.ferris.edu/question/2021/july.htm.

5. "The 'Basket Case' Myth," *Grammarphobia*, updated August 16, 2018, https://www.grammarphobia.com/blog/2014/08/basket-case.html.

6. Margaret Bruchac, "Reclaiming the Word 'Squaw' in the Name of the Ancestors," H-Net Online, December 1, 1999, https://lists.h-net.org/cgi

-bin/logbrowse.pl?trx=vx&list=h-amindian&month=9912&week=a&
msg=//Wt4lIoJcFuIg%2BP975gmg&user=&pw=.

7. Jessica A. Gold, "No, You Shouldn't Call Someone 'Crazy.' But Do We
   Have to Ban the Word Entirely?," *Self*, November 27, 2019, https://www
   .self.com/story/crazy-mental-health-stigma.

8. American Psychological Association, *Publication Manual of the American
   Psychological Association: The Official Guide to APA Style*, 7th ed. (American
   Psychological Association, 2020), 137.

9. Hannah Wallace, "Villages for Unhoused People Are Popping Up in
   More Cities. What's It Like to Live in Them?," *Dwell*, updated May 11, 2023,
   https://www.dwell.com/article/tiny-home-villages-homelessness-oregon
   -747ead25.

10. B. J. Fogg, *Tiny Habits: The Small Changes That Change Everything* (Hough-
    ton Mifflin Harcourt, 2020).

11. "Why Womxn With a 'X'?," Womxn's Center for Success, accessed June
    29, 2023, https://womxnscenter.uci.edu/why-womxn-with-a-x/.

12. Yara Simón, "Latino, Hispanic, Latinx, Chicano: The History Behind the
    Terms," History, updated September 25, 2023, https://www.history.com
    /news/hispanic-latino-latinx-chicano-background.

13. Rachel Hatzipanagos, "'Latinx' Not a Preferred Term Among Hispanics,
    Survey Says," *The Seattle Times*, August 17, 2020, https://www.seattle
    times.com/nation-world/latinx-not-a-preferred-term-among-hispanics
    -survey-says/.

14. John McWhorter, "Why 'Latinx' Can't Catch On," *The Atlantic*, Decem-
    ber 23, 2019, https://www.theatlantic.com/ideas/archive/2019/12/why
    -latinx-cant-catch-on/603943/.

15. Mario Carrasco, "'Hispanic' Preferred Over 'Latinx' When Describing
    Ethnicity," *The Marketing Insider*, July 1, 2020, https://www.mediapost
    .com/publications/article/353227/hispanic-preferred-over-latinx-when
    -describing.html.

16. Joseph Contreras, "Nobody in Miami Says 'Latinx,'" *The Wall Street Jour-
    nal*, February 8, 2023, https://www.wsj.com/articles/nobody-in-miami
    -says-latinx-florida-gender-neutral-term-latino-latina-hispanic-miami
    -newspaper-pronouns-11675866460.

17. Tess Garcia, "Latine vs Latinx? What Young People of Latin American
    Descent Think of These Terms," *Teen Vogue*, October 12, 2022, https://
    www.teenvogue.com/story/latine-vs-latinx-what-young-people-think.

18. "Let's Talk About Latine," Call Me Latine, accessed June 29, 2023, https://
    callmelatine.wordpress.com/.

19. Trevor A. Branch & Danika Kleiber, "Should We Call Them Fishers or Fishermen?," *Fish and Fisheries* 18, no. 1 (January 2017): 114–27, https://doi.org/10.1111/faf.12130.

### Chapter Three: *Practice*

1. Michelle Alexander, *The New Jim Crow: Mass Incarceration in the Age of Colorblindness* (The New Press, 2020).
2. Steve Bien-Aimé, "Rethinking Courtesy Titles in Obituaries," Conscious Style Guide, March 20, 2019, https://consciousstyleguide.com/rethinking-courtesy-titles-in-obituaries/.
3. Jonathan Blitzer, "Baseball Campaign Puts the Accent on Spanish Names," *The New York Times*, August 6, 2016, https://www.nytimes.com/2016/08/07/sports/baseball/eduardo-nunez-putting-accent-on-spanish-names.html.
4. April Dembosky, "California Gives Transgender People Right to Determine Sex Listed on Death Certificate," KQED, updated June 22, 2015, https://www.kqed.org/stateofhealth/18328/new-bill-would-give-transgender-people-more-control-over-death-certificates.
5. Orion Rummler, " 'They're Erased': When Trans People Are Misgendered After Death, the Consequences Extend Beyond Paper," The 19th, January 11, 2023, https://19thnews.org/2023/01/trans-people-misgendering-death-certificates/.
6. "Beyond Red vs. Blue: The Political Typology," Pew Research Center, November 9, 2021, https://www.pewresearch.org/politics/2021/11/09/beyond-red-vs-blue-the-political-typology-2/.
7. Daniel King, "How Language Is Deployed as a Weapon of War," *Mother Jones*, February 25, 2020, https://www.motherjones.com/media/2020/02/how-language-is-deployed-as-a-weapon-of-war/.
8. Lawrence B. Glickman, "The Racist Politics of the English Language," *Boston Review*, November 26, 2018, https://www.bostonreview.net/articles/lawrence-glickman-racially-tinged/.
9. "Why We Say 'Disability,' Not 'Special Needs' — The Mighty Explains," The Mighty, updated October 5, 2023, https://themighty.com/topic/disability/disability-not-special-needs-tme/.
10. Tracy Clark-Flory, "Jeffrey Epstein and the Oxymoron of 'Underage Women,' " *Jezebel*, July 10, 2019, https://jezebel.com/jeffrey-epstein-and-the-oxymoron-of-underage-women-1836247451.
   Jacob Bernstein, "How Did Scott Borgerson Get Mixed Up With Ghislaine Maxwell?," *The New York Times*, updated November 24, 2020, https://www.nytimes.com/2020/08/11/style/who-is-scott-borgerson-ghislaine-maxwell.html.

11. "Why Language Matters: Why We Should Never Use 'Child Pornography' and Always Say Child Sexual Abuse Material," National Society for the Prevention of Cruelty to Children, updated January 30, 2023, https://learning.nspcc.org.uk/news/why-language-matters/child-sexual-abuse-material.

12. Jessica Pressler, "Maybe She Had So Much Money She Just Lost Track of It," *The Cut*, updated February 8, 2022, https://www.thecut.com/article/how-anna-delvey-tricked-new-york.html.

13. Calder McHugh, "Did Sam Bankman-Fried Just End the Era of the Boy Genius?," *Politico*, February 10, 2023, https://www.politico.com/news/magazine/2023/02/10/sam-bankman-fried-crypto-image-00081637.

14. American Library Association, accessed August 29, 2023, https://www.ala.org/ala/protoolsbucket/usersvcsbucket/youngadultbucket/youngadult.htm.

15. Doha Madani, "New York Times Writer's Tweet About Mirai Nagasu Sparks Controversy," *HuffPost*, February 12, 2018, https://www.huffpost.com/entry/bari-weiss-mirai-nagasu-twitter-backlash_n_5a82262be4b0892a035213f5.

16. Eric Sorensen, "Asian Groups Attack MSNBC Headline Referring to Kwan—News Web Site Apologizes for Controversial Wording," *The Seattle Times*, March 3, 1998, https://archive.seattletimes.com/archive/?date=19980303&slug=2737594.

17. Katherine Schaeffer and Drew DeSilver, "Immigrants or Children of Immigrants Make Up at Least 12% of 115th Congress," Pew Research Center, August 21, 2018, https://www.pewresearch.org/short-reads/2018/08/21/immigrants-or-children-of-immigrants-make-up-at-least-12-of-congress/.

18. Richard A. Rogers, "From Cultural Exchange to Transculturation: A Review and Reconceptualization of Cultural Appropriation," *Communication Theory* 16, no. 4 (November 2006): 474–503, https://doi.org/10.1111/j.1468-2885.2006.00277.x.

19. "Which Words Did English Take From Other Languages?," Dictionary.com, October 1, 2018, https://www.dictionary.com/e/borrowed-words/.

20. "Native American Relationships to Animals: Not Your 'Spirit Animal,'" National Museum of the American Indian, accessed June 29, 2023, https://americanindian.si.edu/nk360/informational/native-american-spirit-animal.

21. Robin R. R. Gray, "Appropriation (?) of the Month: First Nation Totem Poles," Intellectual Property Issues in Cultural Heritage, April 18, 2013, https://www.sfu.ca/ipinch/outputs/blog/appropriation-month-first-nation-totem-poles/.

22. John R. Rickford, "What Is Ebonics (African American English)?," Linguistic Society of America, accessed June 22, 2023, https://www .linguisticsociety.org/content/what-ebonics-african-american-english.

23. Ishena Robinson, "How Woke Went From 'Black' to 'Bad,'" Legal Defense Fund, August 26, 2022, https://www.naacpldf.org/woke-black -bad/.

24. Sydnee Thompson, "So Much Modern Slang Is AAVE. Here's How Language Appropriation Erases the Influence of Black Culture," *Buzz-Feed News*, September 7, 2021, https://www.buzzfeednews.com/article /sydneethompson/aave-language-appropriation.

25. Emma Veidt, "The North Face Is Renaming Its 'Sherpa' Fleece," *Backpacker*, updated October 4, 2022, https://www.backpacker.com/news-and-events /news/the-north-face-is-renaming-its-sherpa-fleece/.

26. Suhag Shukla, "The Power of Namaste," Hindu American Foundation, March 4, 2020, https://www.hinduamerican.org/blog/the-power-of -namaste.

27. Elizabeth A. McAlister, "Vodou," *Britannica*, updated September 29, 2023, https://www.britannica.com/topic/Vodou.

28. Denise-Marie Ordway, "Want to Reach Skeptics? Researchers Suggest Leaving the Term 'Climate Change' Out of Some News Coverage," *The Journalist's Resource*, May 28, 2022, https://journalistsresource.org /environment/science-skeptics-climate-change-news/.

29. Naseem S. Miller, "6 Tips for Covering COVID-19 Vaccine Hesitancy," *The Journalist's Resource*, September 7, 2021, https://journalistsresource .org/health/6-tips-for-covering-vaccine-hesitancy/.

30. Krishnendu Ray, *The Ethnic Restaurateur* (Bloomsbury Academic, 2016).

31. Henry Fuhrmann, "Drop the Hyphen in *Asian American*," Conscious Style Guide, January 23, 2018, https://consciousstyleguide.com/drop-hyphen -asian-american/.

32. Fuhrmann, "Drop the Hyphen in *Asian American*."

33. Gary J. Gates, "How Many People Are Lesbian, Gay, Bisexual, and Trans-gender?," Williams Institute, April 2011, https://williamsinstitute.law .ucla.edu/publications/how-many-people-lgbt/.

34. Jeffrey M. Jones, "LGBT Identification Rises to 5.6% in Latest U.S. Esti-mate," Gallup, February 24, 2021, https://news.gallup.com/poll/329708 /lgbt-identification-rises-latest-estimate.aspx.

35. Jennifer L. Truman and Rachel E. Morgan, "Violent Victimization by Sexual Orientation and Gender Identity, 2017–2020," US Department of Justice, Office of Justice Programs, Bureau of Justice Statistics, June 2022,

https://bjs.ojp.gov/library/publications/violent-victimization-sexual
-orientation-and-gender-identity-2017-2020.

36. Julia Taylor et al., "Bisexual Mental Health: 'Findings From the 'Who I Am' Study,'" *Australian Journal of General Practice* 48, no. 3 (March 2019): 138–44, https://doi.org/10.31128/AJGP-06-18-4615.

37. Taylor et al., "Bisexual Mental Health."

38. Brian A. Feinstein et al., "A Qualitative Examination of Bisexual Identity Invalidation and Its Consequences for Wellbeing, Identity, and Relationships," *Journal of Bisexuality* 19, no. 4 (October 2019), 461–82, https://doi .org/10.1080/15299716.2019.1671295.

39. Aubrey Gordon, "I'm a Fat Activist. I Don't Use the Word *Fatphobia*. Here's Why," *Self*, March 29, 2021, https://www.self.com/story/fat-activist -fatphobia.

40. Hadley Freeman, "Michael J Fox: 'Nobody Pities Me and That's Great. I Couldn't Stand It,'" *The Guardian*, October 6, 2013, https://www .theguardian.com/culture/2013/oct/06/michael-j-fox-sitcom-parkinsons -alcoholism-divorce.

41. Robin Jeshion, "Pride and Prejudiced: On the Reclamation of Slurs," *Grazer Philosophische Studien* 97, no. 1 (2020): 106–37, https://doi.org/10.1163 /18756735-09701007.

42. Barbara Wallraff, "May I Have a Word: Another Way to Say 'Trump,'" *The Boston Globe*, January 25, 2022, https://www.bostonglobe.com/2022 /01/25/opinion/may-i-have-word-another-way-say-trump/.

43. Bruchac, "Reclaiming the Word 'Squaw.'"

44. Adrienne M. Selko, "Is the Term Blue Collar Outdated?," *IndustryWeek*, June 6, 2019, https://www.industryweek.com/talent/article/22027706/is -the-term-blue-collar-outdated.

45. Alan Mayne, *Slums: The History of a Global Injustice* (Reaktion Books, 2017).

46. Jake Blumgart, "Should We Retire the Word 'Slum'?," *Bloomberg*, October 10, 2017, https://www.bloomberg.com/news/articles/2017-10-10/the-case -for-retiring-the-word-slum.

47. Marc Silver, "If You Shouldn't Call It the Third World, What Should You Call It?," NPR, January 4, 2015, https://www.npr.org/sections/goatsandsoda /2015/01/04/372684438/if-you-shouldnt-call-it-the-third-world-what -should-you-call-it.

48. Margaret M. Quinlan and Bethany Johnson, "Why One Mom Battles to Change the Term 'Incompetent Cervix,'" *Psychology Today*, May 12, 2021, https://www.psychologytoday.com/us/blog/medical-humanities

-mamas/202105/why-one-mom-battles-change-the-term-incompetent
-cervix.

49. "Community and Culture—Frequently Asked Questions," National
Association of the Deaf, accessed June 29, 2023, https://www.nad.org
/resources/american-sign-language/community-and-culture-frequently
-asked-questions/.

50. "Low Vision and Legal Blindness Terms and Descriptions," American
Foundation for the Blind, accessed August 31, 2023, https://www.afb
.org/blindness-and-low-vision/eye-conditions/low-vision-and-legal
-blindness-terms-and-descriptions.

51. "Community and Culture," National Association of the Deaf.

52. Elliott Almond, "Olympics: Stanford's Simone Manuel and Michael
Phelps Make History," *The Mercury News*, updated January 11, 2018,
https://www.mercurynews.com/2016/08/11/olympics-stanfords-simone
-manuel-and-michael-phelps-make-history/.

53. Arianne Shahvisi, "'Men Are Trash': The Surprisingly Philosophical
Story Behind an Internet Punchline," *Prospect*, August 19, 2019, https://
www.prospectmagazine.co.uk/ideas/philosophy/39112/men-are-trash
-the-surprisingly-philosophical-story-behind-an-internet-punchline.

54. Lucienne Spencer and Havi Carel, "'Isn't Everyone a Little OCD?' The
Epistemic Harms of Wrongful Depathologization," *Philosophy of Medicine* 2, no. 1 (April 2021): 1–18, https://doi.org/10.5195/pom.2021.19.

55. Douglas S. Massey and Karen A. Pren, "Unintended Consequences of US
Immigration Policy: Explaining the Post-1965 Surge From Latin America," *Population and Development Review* 38, no. 1 (March 2012): 1–29,
https://doi.org/10.1111/j.1728-4457.2012.00470.x.

56. Jared Goyette, "A Historically Xenophobic Metaphor Has Been Used by
Trump, Limbaugh, Obama—and Us?," *The World*, January 29, 2016,
https://theworld.org/stories/2016-01-29/historically-xenophobic-metaphor
-used-trump-limbaugh-obama-and-us.

57. Hanna Lustig, "Teens on TikTok Are Exposing a Generational Rift
Between Parents and Kids Over How They Treat Black Lives Matter Protests," *Insider*, June 3, 2020, https://www.insider.com/tiktok-george-floyd
-black-lives-matter-teens-parents-racist-views-2020-6.

58. "Israel's Religiously Divided Society," Pew Research Center, March 8,
2016, https://www.pewresearch.org/religion/2016/03/08/jewish-beliefs
-and-practices/.

59. "U.S. Public Becoming Less Religious," Pew Research Center, November 3, 2015, https://www.pewresearch.org/religion/2015/11/03/chapter
-2-religious-practices-and-experiences/.

60. "Not All Women Gained the Vote in 1920," *American Experience*, July 6, 2020, https://www.pbs.org/wgbh/americanexperience/features/vote-not -all-women-gained-right-to-vote-in-1920/.

61. Theresa Tamkins, "Here's Why Experts Think Suicides Dropped During the Pandemic," *BuzzFeed News*, updated January 28, 2022, https://www.buzzfeed news.com/article/theresatamkins/suicide-rates-dropped-pandemic.

62. Eric Todisco, "TV Host Issues Emotional Apology After Saying Her Black Co-Anchor Looks Like a Gorilla," *People*, August 28, 2019, https:// people.com/tv/tv-host-apologizes-saying-black-coanchor-gorilla/.

63. Natasha Noman, "Sacha Baron Cohen and the Other Oscar Moments That Had Us Groaning," *Mic*, February 29, 2016, republished on *Yahoo News*, https://news.yahoo.com/sacha-baron-cohen-other-oscar-142600814.html.

64. "Dogs in a Chinese Restaurant? It's Not What You Think," *Angry Asian Man*, February 21, 2017, https://blog.angryasianman.com/2017/02/dogs -in-chinese-restaurant-its-not-what.html.

65. Dustin Vogt, "Coroner Identifies Woman Shot and Killed in Officer-Involved Shooting," WAVE, updated May 16, 2020, https://www.wave3 .com/2020/03/15/coroner-identifies-woman-shot-killed-officer-involved -shooting/.

66. Christopher Bucktin, "George Floyd Protests Across US Hijacked by White Provocateurs to Start Riots," *Mirror*, updated June 1, 2020, https:// www.mirror.co.uk/news/us-news/george-floyd-protests-hijacked-white -22116897.

67. "'Chink in the Armor'? Really, ESPN?," *Angry Asian Man*, February 17, 2012, https://blog.angryasianman.com/2012/02/chink-in-armor-really-espn .html.

68. Jordan Valinsky, "Ulta Beauty Apologizes for 'Very Insensitive' Email About Kate Spade," CNN, May 3, 2022, https://www.cnn.com/2022/05/03 /business/kate-spade-ulta-email/index.html.

69. "An Introduction to Content Warnings and Trigger Warnings," University of Michigan College of Literature, Science, and the Arts, downloaded June 29, 2023, https://sites.lsa.umich.edu/inclusive-teaching-sandbox /wp-content/uploads/sites/853/2021/02/An-Introduction-to-Content -Warnings-and-Trigger-Warnings-Draft.pdf.

70. Tien Nguyen, "Why We Should Examine Our Culinary Vocabulary," Conscious Style Guide, March 29, 2018, https://consciousstyleguide.com /why-we-should-examine-our-culinary-vocabulary/.

71. "Thinx Are Toxic, Olive Oil Fraud & Self-Destructing TVs," *The Wreck List*, January 18, 2023, https://www.thewrecklist.com/p/olive-oil-fraud -self-destructing.

72. Edward Alwood, "A Matter of Shame," *The Investigative Reporters and Editors Journal*, fourth quarter 2021.

73. Clo S, "What Happened When I Stopped Using Emojis," *This Too Shall Grow*, accessed June 29, 2023, https://thistooshallgrow.com/blog/emoji -stop.

74. Tess Sharpe, "Content Warnings for 6 Times We Almost Kissed," Tumblr, May 23, 2022, https://www.tumblr.com/sharpegirl/685079564101238784 /content-warnings-for-6-times-we-almost-kissed.

75. "Sample Syllabus Language," Claremont Colleges Center for Teaching and Learning, accessed June 29, 2023, https://colleges.claremont.edu/ctl /resources/ctl-created-resources/sample-syllabus-language/.

76. "Sweet_Anita," Twitch, accessed June 29, 2023, https://www.twitch.tv /Sweet_Anita/about.

77. "Not to Be Trusted: Dangerous Levels of Inaccuracy in TV Crime Reporting in NYC," Color of Change, March 2015, https://colorofchange .org/newsaccuracyratings/.

78. Meg Anderson and Nick McMillan, "1,000 People Have Been Charged for the Capitol Riot. Here's Where Their Cases Stand," NPR, March 25, 2023, https://www.npr.org/2023/03/25/1165022885/1000-defendants-january -6-capitol-riot.

79. Amber Jamieson and Julia Reinstein, "At Least 10 People Have Been Killed in a Mass Shooting at a Supermarket in Buffalo," *BuzzFeed News*, updated May 15, 2022, https://www.buzzfeednews.com/article /amberjamieson/buffalo-tops-supermarket-mass-shooting.

80. Robin DiAngelo, "White People Are Still Raised to Be Racially Illiterate. If We Don't Recognize the System, Our Inaction Will Uphold It," *Think*, NBC News Digital, September 16, 2018, https://www.nbcnews.com /think/opinion/white-people-are-still-raised-be-racially-illiterate-if-we -ncna906646.

81. Tamkins, "Here's Why Experts Think Suicides Dropped During the Pandemic."

82. George Lakoff, *The All New Don't Think of an Elephant! Know Your Values and Frame the Debate* (Chelsea Green Publishing, 2014).

83. "Officers Kill Man With No Active Warrants at Wrong House," WMC Action News 5, updated July 26, 2017, https://www.actionnews5.com /story/35967817/officers-kill-man-with-no-active-warrants-at-wrong -house/.

84. *Cultural Competence Handbook*, National Association of Hispanic Journalists, March 2021.

85. Dana Nuccitelli, "Survey Finds 97% of Climate Science Papers Agree Warming Is Man-Made," *The Guardian*, May 16, 2013, https://www.theguardian.com/environment/climate-consensus-97-per-cent/2013/may/16/climate-change-scienceofclimatechange.

86. Robert S. Eshelman, "The Danger of Fair and Balanced," *Columbia Journalism Review*, accessed June 29, 2023, https://archives.cjr.org/essay/the_danger_of_fair_and_balance.php.

87. Rosie Gray, "Trump Defends White-Nationalist Protesters: 'Some Very Fine People on Both Sides,'" *The Atlantic*, August 15, 2017, https://www.theatlantic.com/politics/archive/2017/08/trump-defends-white-nationalist-protesters-some-very-fine-people-on-both-sides/537012/.

88. Max Witynski, "False Balance in News Coverage of Climate Change Makes It Harder to Address the Crisis," *Northwestern Now*, July 22, 2022, https://news.northwestern.edu/stories/2022/07/false-balance-reporting-climate-change-crisis/.

89. Sarah Mervosh, "Florida Scoured Math Textbooks for 'Prohibited Topics.' Next Up: Social Studies," *The New York Times*, updated March 20, 2023, https://www.nytimes.com/2023/03/16/us/florida-textbooks-african-american-history.html.

90. "It Is Not Possible for One Man to Hold Another Man Down in the Ditch Without Staying Down There With Him," Quote Investigator, December 8, 2019, https://quoteinvestigator.com/2019/12/08/hold/.

91. Booker T. Washington, *The Story of the Negro: The Rise of the Race From Slavery* (Doubleday, Page & Company, 1909), 124.

92. American Civil Liberties Union (@ACLU), on Twitter, September 18, 2021, https://twitter.com/ACLU/status/1439259891064004610.

93. Louise Melling, "For Justice Ginsburg, Abortion Was About Equality," American Civil Liberties Union, September 23, 2020, https://www.aclu.org/news/reproductive-freedom/for-justice-ginsburg-abortion-was-about-equality.

94. Desmond Butler, Amy Brittain, and Alice Li, "Female Bodybuilders Describe Widespread Sexual Exploitation," *The Washington Post*, updated October 28, 2022, https://www.washingtonpost.com/investigations/interactive/2022/women-bodybuilding-ifbb-pro-porn/.

95. Hawai'i Visitors and Convention Bureau, accessed August 31, 2023, https://www.hvcb.org/.

96. Madelyn Burbank, "What You Need to Know About Teen Dating Violence," Daily Herald, February 10, 2024, https://www.dailyherald.com/20240210/health-and-fitness/what-you-need-to-know-about-teen-dating-violence-2/.

97. "BuzzFeed Style Guide," *BuzzFeed News*, updated March 8, 2023, https://www.buzzfeed.com/buzzfeednews/buzzfeed-style-guide.

98. "Disaster Distress Helpline," Substance Abuse and Mental Health Services Administration, updated June 9, 2023, https://www.samhsa.gov/find-help/disaster-distress-helpline.

99. Sari M. van Anders, "Beyond Sexual Orientation: Integrating Gender/Sex and Diverse Sexualities via Sexual Configurations Theory," *Archives of Sexual Behavior* 44, no. 5 (July 2015): 1177–213, https://doi.org/10.1007/s10508-015-0490-8.

100. Michael G. McDunnah, "Doctor He, She, or They? Changing Gender, and Language, in *Doctor Who*," Conscious Style Guide, January 16, 2019, https://consciousstyleguide.com/doctor-he-she-or-they-changing-gender-and-language-in-doctor-who/.

101. Miriam Miyagi, Eartha Mae Guthman, and Simón(e) Dow-Kuang Sun, "Transgender Rights Rely on Inclusive Language," *Science* 374, no. 6575 (2021): 1568–69, https://doi.org/10.1126/science.abn3759.

102. Harrison Ray, "Cable News Networks Obsessed Over Biden's Age While Overwhelmingly Ignoring Trump's," Media Matters for America, June 22, 2023, https://www.mediamatters.org/joe-biden/cable-news-networks-obsessed-over-bidens-age-while-overwhelmingly-ignoring-trumps.

103. Chimamanda Ngozi Adichie, "The Danger of a Single Story," TEDGlobal 2009, July 2009, https://www.ted.com/talks/chimamanda_ngozi_adichie_the_danger_of_a_single_story.

104. "Guidance on Web Accessibility and the ADA," US Department of Justice Civil Rights Division, March 18, 2022, https://www.ada.gov/resources/web-guidance/.

105. "The WebAIM Million," WebAIM, updated March 29, 2023, https://webaim.org/projects/million/.

106. "Disability Language Style Guide," National Center on Disability and Journalism, updated August 2021, https://ncdj.org/style-guide/.

107. Folklore Salon & Barber, accessed May 13, 2023, https://salonfolklore.com/.

108. "Bisexual FAQ," Human Rights Campaign, accessed June 29, 2023, https://www.hrc.org/resources/bisexual-faq.

109. Helen Green and Ash Riddington, "Gender Inclusive Language in Perinatal Services: Mission Statement and Rationale," Brighton and Sussex University Hospitals, December 22, 2020, https://www.liverpool.ac.uk/media/livacuk/schoolofmedicine/leo/documents/Gender-inclusive-language-in-perinatal-services,(2).pdf.

110. Kristen Harmon, "On Deaf Literature," *Bloomsbury Literary Studies*, January 18, 2019, https://bloomsburyliterarystudiesblog.com/2019/01/on-deaf-literature.html.

111. Willem Hollmann, "Five Things People Get Wrong About Standard English," *The Conversation*, October 8, 2021, https://theconversation.com/five-things-people-get-wrong-about-standard-english-168969.

112. Joshua J. Mark, "Color in Ancient Egypt," *World History Encyclopedia*, January 8, 2017, https://www.worldhistory.org/article/999/color-in-ancient-egypt/.

113. Elisabeth Sherman, "Why Does 'Yellow Filter' Keep Popping Up in American Movies?," Matador Network, April 27, 2020, https://matadornetwork.com/read/yellow-filter-american-movies/.

114. Samantha Schmidt, "Kellogg's Apologizes for Lone Brown Corn Pop on Cereal Box," *The Washington Post*, October 26, 2017, https://www.washingtonpost.com/news/morning-mix/wp/2017/10/26/kelloggs-apologizes-for-lone-brown-corn-pop-on-cereal-box/.

115. Christine Ma, "Picture Book Images and Unconscious Bias," Conscious Style Guide, April 13, 2022, https://consciousstyleguide.com/picture-book-images-and-unconscious-bias/.

116. "Anne Hathaway Apologises for Portrayal of Limb Difference in The Witches," BBC, November 6, 2020, https://www.bbc.com/news/entertainment-arts-54838201.

117. Maya Terhune, "A Good Little Monkey: *Curious George*'s Undercurrent of White Dominance and the Series' Continued Popularity," Boston University's College of Arts and Sciences Writing Program, accessed June 29, 2023, https://www.bu.edu/writingprogram/journal/past-issues/issue-7/terhune/.

118. Alexander Abad-Santos, "Ursula Liang vs. *Breakfast at Tiffany's* Screening," *The Atlantic*, July 14, 2011, https://www.theatlantic.com/culture/archive/2011/07/ursula-liang-vs-breakfast-tiffanys/352862/.

119. Katy Gagliardi, "Facebook Captions: Kindness, or Inspiration Porn?," *M/C Journal* 20, no. 3 (2017), https://doi.org/10.5204/mcj.1258.

120. Rachel E. Greenspan, "People Keep Sharing the Video of George Floyd. Some Activists and Mental Health Professionals Are Calling It 'Pain Porn' and Begging Them to Stop," *Business Insider*, May 29, 2020, https://www.businessinsider.com/george-floyd-video-activists-are-begging-people-stop-posting-2020-5.

121. Andrew Pulrang, "3 Things Non-Disabled People Should Do Before Calling Out Ableism," *Forbes*, December 31, 2022, https://www.forbes

.com/sites/andrewpulrang/2022/12/31/3-things-non-disabled-people -should-do-before-calling-out-ableism/.

122. Anne Quito, "Karate, Wonton, Chow Fun: The End of 'Chop Suey' Fonts," CNN, April 8, 2021, https://www.cnn.com/style/article/chop-suey -fonts-hyphenated/index.html.

123. "Archived Posts—April 2022," *Angry Asian Man*, April 17, 2002, https:// blog.angryasianman.com/2002/04/archived-posts-april-2002.html.

124. "Speak Up: Responding to Everyday Bigotry," Southern Poverty Law Center, January 26, 2015, https://www.splcenter.org/20150125/speak -responding-everyday-bigotry.

125. "Speak Up: Responding to Everyday Bigotry," Southern Poverty Law Center.

126. Mia Mingus, "The Four Parts of Accountability & How to Give a Genuine Apology," Leaving Evidence, December 18, 2019, https://leavingevidence.wordpress.com/2019/12/18/how-to-give-a-good-apology-part-1 -the-four-parts-of-accountability/.

### Chapter Four: *Pause*

1. Shereen Marisol Meraji, Natalie Escobar, and Kumari Devarajan, "Is It Time to Say R.I.P. to 'POC'?," *Code Switch*, September 30, 2020, https:// www.npr.org/2020/09/29/918418825/is-it-time-to-say-r-i-p-to-p-o-c.

2. Emily A. Margolis, "A Seat in the Flight Deck: Recognizing and Replacing Biases With Gender Inclusive Language," National Air and Space Museum, March 30, 2021, https://airandspace.si.edu/stories/editorial/seat -flight-deck-gender-inclusive-language.

3. "What's a Festival Without a Controversy?," Michigan Womyn's Music Festival, accessed May 19, 2023, https://www.michfest.com/Updates /controversy/.

4. Denise-Marie Ordway, "Want to Reach Skeptics? Researchers Suggest Leaving the Term 'Climate Change' Out of Some News Coverage," *The Journalist's Resource*, May 28, 2022, https://journalistsresource.org /environment/science-skeptics-climate-change-news/.

5. Ken Miguel, "A Message From Our National Board President," NLGJA: The Association of LGBTQ+ Journalists, February 15, 2023, https:// www.nlgja.org/blog/2023/02/a-message-from-our-national-board -president/.

6. Megan Leonhardt, "23% of Workers Say Employers Are Offering New Mental Health Benefits. But Is It Enough?," *Fortune*, April 29, 2022, https:// fortune.com/well/2022/04/29/23-percent-of-workers-say-employers-offer -mental-health-benefits/.

7. "Traditional Chinese Medicine," *Britannica*, updated October 27, 2023, https://britannica.com/science/traditional-Chinese-medicine.

8. Nick Ortner, *The Tapping Solution: A Revolutionary System for Stress-Free Living* (Hay House, 2013).

9. "Emotional Freedom Technique (EFT)," Kaiser Permanente, updated June 25, 2023, https://healthy.kaiserpermanente.org/health-wellness /health-encyclopedia/he.emotional-freedom-technique-eft.acl9225.

10. Daniel A. Monti et al., "Neuro Emotional Technique Effects on Brain Physiology in Cancer Patients With Traumatic Stress Symptoms: Preliminary Findings," *Journal of Cancer Survivorship* 11, no. 4 (August 2017): 438–46, https://doi.org/10.1007/s11764-017-0601-8.

11. Alice E. Molloy, *In Other Words*, as quoted by Rosalie Maggio, Quotations by Women, accessed September 10, 2023, https://quotationsbywomen .com/authorq/21035/.

**Chapter Five: *Persuade***

1. German Lopez, "Research Says There Are Ways to Reduce Racial Bias. Calling People Racist Isn't One of Them," *Vox*, updated July 30, 2018, https://www.vox.com/identities/2016/11/15/13595508/racism-research -study-trump.

2. Kristina M. Launey and Minh N. Vu, "Plaintiffs Set a New Record for Website Accessibility Lawsuit Filings in 2022," ADA Title III News & Insights, January 23, 2023, https://www.adatitleiii.com/2023/01/plaintiffs -set-a-new-record-for-website-accessibility-lawsuit-filings-in-2022/.

3. "Fuck (v.)," Online Etymology Dictionary, accessed May 30, 2023, https:// www.etymonline.com/search?q=fuck.

# SELECTED BIBLIOGRAPHY AND FURTHER READING

American Psychological Association. *Publication Manual of the American Psychological Association: The Official Guide to APA Style.* 7th ed. American Psychological Association, 2020. Also available at https://apastyle.apa.org/.

The Associated Press. *The Associated Press Stylebook.* 57th ed. The Associated Press, 2024. Also available at https://apstylebook.com/.

Briscoe, Felecia, Gilberto Arriaza, and Rosemary C. Henze. *The Power of Talk: How Words Change Our Lives.* Corwin, 2009.

Fogg, B. J. *Tiny Habits: The Small Changes That Change Everything.* Houghton Mifflin Harcourt, 2020.

Imani, Blair. *Read This to Get Smarter: About Race, Class, Gender, Disability and More.* Ten Speed Press, 2021.

Lakoff, George. *The All New Don't Think of an Elephant! Know Your Values and Frame the Debate.* Chelsea Green Publishing, 2014.

Stollznow, Karen. *On the Offensive: Prejudice in Language Past and Present.* Cambridge University Press, 2020.

Thich Nhat Hanh. *The Art of Communicating.* HarperOne, 2013.

University of Chicago Press. *The Chicago Manual of Style.* 18th ed. University of Chicago Press, 2024. Also available at https://www.chicago manualofstyle.org/.

Yoshino, Kenji and David Glasgow. *Say the Right Thing: How to Talk About Identity, Diversity, and Justice.* Atria Books, 2023.

# CREDITS

LITTLE, BROWN SPARK
VICE PRESIDENT, PUBLISHER, AND EDITOR IN CHIEF
Tracy Behar

ART AND DESIGN
Julianna Lee
Judy Wings

COPYEDITOR AND PROOFREADERS
Crystal Shelley
Barbara Jatkola
Pamela Marshall

EDITORIAL SUPPORT
Karina Leon

INDEXER
Heather Laskey

MARKETING
Jessica Chun

PRODUCTION COORDINATOR
Erin Cain

PRODUCTION EDITOR
Betsy Uhrig

PUBLICITY
Gabby Leporati

# INDEX

# Index

# ABOUT THE AUTHOR

Award-winning writer and editor Karen Yin is the force behind Conscious Style Guide (which was a website before it inspired a book) and *The Conscious Language Newsletter*. She also founded the Editors of Color Database, one of *Writer's Digest*'s Best Websites for Writers 2023, and *AP vs. Chicago*, a humorous blog for anyone who "gives a dollar sign, ampersand, exclamation point, and pound sign about style." Named editor of the year by ACES: The Society for Editing in 2017, Yin has served on the *Chicago Manual of Style* advisory board and contributed to *The Associated Press Stylebook*. Her children's books include *Whole Whale, So Not Ghoul, Doug the Pug and the Kindness Crew,* and *Nice to Eat You*. Yin is writing another book at this exact moment somewhere in Southern California.

KarenYin.com
ConsciousStyleGuide.com